FLYING SAUCERS ARE EVERYWHERE

FLYING SAUCERS ARE EVERYWHERE

TOM McHUGH
ILLUSTRATED BY JOHN KLOSS

Prometheus Books
59 John Glenn Drive
Amherst, NewYork 14228-2197

Published 1995 by Prometheus Books

Flying Saucers Are Everywhere. Copyright © 1995 by Tom McHugh. Illustrations copyright © 1995 by John Kloss. All rights reserved. No part of this publication may be reproduced, stored in a retrieval system, or transmitted in any form or by any means, electronic, mechanical, photocopying, recording, or otherwise, without prior written permission of the publisher, except in the case of brief quotations embodied in critical articles and reviews. Inquiries should be addressed to Prometheus Books, 59 John Glenn Drive, Amherst, New York 14228-2197, 716-691-0133. FAX: 716-691-0137.

Library of Congress Cataloging-in-Publication Data

McHugh, Tom, 1958–
    Flying saucers are everywhere / Tom McHugh ; illustrated by John Kloss.
       p.   cm.
    ISBN 978-0-87975-982-7 (pbk.)
    1. Flying saucers—humor. 2. Unidentified flying objects-Sightings and encounters—Humor. 3. Abduction—Humor. I. Kloss, John. II. Title.
PN6162.M344   1995
818'.5407—dc20   95-7389
                                                                     CIP

For my mother, who helped me develop my imagination, but who should not be blamed for the ways I sometimes use it.

Contents

Preface and Acknowledgments		9
Introduction		11
One.	Wheelbarrows of the Gods	15
Two.	Flying Saucers in the Bible	31
Three.	What They Didn't Tell You in History Class about Flying Saucers	43
Four.	Modern UFO Sightings and Close Encounters in Hickstown	53
Five.	Those Mysterious Crop Circles	63
Six.	Abduction by the Aliens: The Bumpkin Story	71
Seven.	Invasion of the Cricket Men and Other Alien Species	83
Eight.	The Big Government Cover-Up and Radar-Resistant Cheese	99
Nine.	The Bermuda Triangle and Other Dangerous Polygons	111
Ten.	Flying Saucers in the World Today	129

Preface and Acknowledgments

The surgeon general requires me to warn you that the book you are about to read is a parody. It is based on incidents which, as far as the author knows, have never taken place, and facts which were intentionally made up out of thin air. Anyone who takes anything in this book seriously could be at risk of extreme gullibility and excessive foolhardiness, and is likely to become the butt of many jokes.

Now that the legalities are out of the way, I would like to thank some of the people who inspired and encouraged me while I wrote this book. Madeline Di Maggio and her Palo Alto-based writer's workshop were very helpful, patient, and constructive in their critiques. Jerry McCarthy was especially encouraging in his confidence that there would be a market for a flying saucer spoof. The Mutual UFO Network and many other UFO organizations known by such acronyms as APRO, NICAP, and CUFOS have been an inspiration by keeping the faith, sometimes against all odds, and by providing an unending source of saucer stories.

I also owe some gratitude to numerous tacky TV specials and shameless tabloid newspapers for proving time and again that there are no limits to hyperbole or gullibility. Thanks to

Steven Mitchell, Eugene O'Connor, Ann Marie Pellegrino, Jacqueline Cooke, and all the kind folks at Prometheus Books for adding their talents to this book. Thanks as well to Jeanette Campbell, Carol Perry, Paulette Vogler, Diana Barnes, Carol Bain, Penny Rozzi, Deborah Todd, Pete Stonebridge, Erin Briggs, Johnnye Gibson, Michael Kennedy, and Terry Merchant.

In addition I thank all my friends from Federal Systems Division for their encouragement and, most of all, I thank my family, especially my mother, for a lot of valuable encouragement and suggestions.

Introduction

- In 1905 a Swiss patent clerk named ALBERT EINSTEIN published his THEORY OF RELATIVITY, which contained the equation:
$$E = MC^2.$$
- In the mid 1940s, American scientists developed the first electronic HIGH-SPEED COMPUTERS that could perform thousands of calculations per second.
- And in 1972 a NUCLEAR-POWERED SUBMARINE was lost, never to be seen again, after it disappeared into THE BERMUDA TRIANGLE.

What do these three facts have in common? They all use CAPITAL LETTERS, they all describe some SENSATIONAL EVENT, and they are all examples of the impressive, scientific-sounding journalism you will be reading in this book.

This book is the result of years of research into the field that is often called UFOlogy (pronounced *hoax*). For the benefit of the gullible layman, for whom this book was written, I will define the term UFOlogy. A UFO is the abbreviation for an "Unidentified Flying Object," known to laymen as Flying

Saucers. "Logy" is an actual word that means heavy and sluggish, but that has nothing to do with UFOlogy as far as I know. *UFOlogy*, therefore, is the study of Unidentified Flying Objects.

A person, such as myself, who participates in the study of UFOs is known as a *UFOlogist*.

A person who doesn't believe in UFOs is called a *spy* and is probably involved in the GOVERNMENT COVER-UP.

A person who buys this book and believes everything in it is called *naive*.

In my work as a UFOlogist, I have traveled to nearly every state in the U.S.A. and to many foreign lands, including Louisiana. I have logged thousands of frequent flier points and collected hundreds of baby hotel soaps all in my devoted effort to get to the bottom of the UFO controversy.

Are UFOs really spaceships carrying visitors from other planets? Are they beings from another dimension that sometimes fly through hyperspace into our universe? Did the government really capture slimy-skinned alien creatures from crashed UFOs, and did it sell their bodies to McDonald's for use in McRib sandwiches? And why do UFOlogists ask so many rhetorical questions? You will find potential answers to these and many more legendary mysteries of the universe in this authoritative volume.

This book, for the first time this publishing season, presents overwhelming evidence that UFOlogists have existed throughout history. It proves that many naive people are convinced the earth is being watched by VISITORS FROM OUTER SPACE, and it strongly suggests that THE U.S. GOVERNMENT is conspiring to COVER UP all evidence that the BERMUDA TRIANGLE is actually a TRAPEZOID.

I did not come upon these historic revelations all at once. It took years of research and a skeptical, scientific mind to discover the truth. I interviewed thousands of amateur astronomers, bird watchers, and town drunks and compared all their testimony. I stayed up all night in rural corn fields to witness spaceship landings and to watch passionate teenagers discover sex. I researched UFO reports from throughout history, read up on all the current paperbacks and watched *Close Encounters of the Third Kind* forty-three times. I studied ancient stone tablets and papyrus scrolls, just in case they contained any information concerning spaceships. I went to UFO workshops to meet contactees and took hallucinogenic drugs that got me so high I didn't need a flying saucer to go to Venus.

By the time my research was complete I had compiled notes on over 97 million individual UFO cases. For the purposes of this book, they have been edited down to just a handful of examples, and a few cartoons; but take my word for it, there were millions. The only possible conclusions that I could come to were that Jack Ruby acted alone, that Jimmy Hoffa is buried in Elvis' grave, and that, above all else, FLYING SAUCERS ARE EVERYWHERE!

One

Wheelbarrows of the Gods

We have all read recent newspaper accounts of UFO sightings. They typically describe everyday folks like you and me who just happen to look up into the sky and see a streak of light, a glowing sphere, or the ghost of their Aunt Frieda. One example is this newspaper clipping from the *Ragloid Weekly*:

> HUCKSTERVILLE, MISSOURI: Local authorities have vehemently denied that Hucksterville is being invaded by UFOs despite dozens of calls about strange lights in the sky. Major Jim-Bob Duffer at the National Guard Armory told the *Ragloid* that he has sent men out to check up on several UFO reports. Duffer said his men haven't seen anything except streaks of light and glowing spheres, which, he says, can be explained as manifestations of the ghost of his Aunt Frieda who has been haunting the town for years.

Most UFO reports are denied by the authorities because of the big GOVERNMENT COVER-UP, but I'll have more to say about that in a later chapter. The point here is that UFOs are often seen in towns with humorous names like Hucksterville.

Flying Saucers Are Everywhere

* * *

How long, you may ask, have UFOs been around? Did they first appear when the ATOMIC BOMB was invented? Were they predicted by EINSTEIN'S THEORY OF RELATIVITY? The truth is, they have been around since the beginning of time. In fact, many disputed scientists theorize that UFOs were responsible for the development of life on Earth. These scientists have shown that the oldest known myths, stories of gods walking among men, are eyewitness accounts of ANCIENT ASTRONAUTS, who had come from OUTER SPACE to check up on the development of PROJECT EARTH.

These legends have been passed down through the ages as imaginative folklore; but if we take a close look at these ancient myths, we can detect some common threads in every one of them. And, since threads weren't even invented until centuries later, we can only assume that they were brought to the ancient scribes from outer space.

Let's look at one of these tales and see what kind of clues we can find. The oldest known myth is a story called The Epic of Gilgamesh. It was written on clay tablets in a form of writing called *cuneiform* (literally: random markings). The epic tells the story of King Gilgamesh of the Gilgamites, a dwarfish people with dirt between their toes who grew lapis-lazuli crops between the Tyrannic and Euphemistic rivers.

According to the epic, one day King Gilgamesh was yoking his oxen, as he was wont to do when there were no young maidens around for him to yoke, and a winged serpent flew down from the heavens and challenged him with a puzzle.

"How many Celestial Beasts doth it take to changeth a light bulb?" the serpent asked?

"Harketh!" cried King Gilgamesh, "what, wherefore the heck, is a light bulb?"

"Harketh thyself," retorted the serpent, "it is that instrument by which the gods maketh the light that allowest us to see."

"If that is so," replied Gilgamesh, "then no Celestial Beast may changeth such a thing. Only the gods wouldst do so in their FLYING SAUCERS."

"Thou art truly a wise king," replied the serpent, after which it turned Gilgamesh into a boll weevil.

If one takes a close look at this archaic myth, one begins to wonder how the ancient chroniclers ever got through it with a straight face. But one also has to ask how these people from the Middle East knew of the existence of the boll weevil, a beetle that only exists in Texas and Mexico. Did they get this knowledge from highly advanced space travelers?

I took a trip to Mexico to look into this cosmic mystery. The famous Swiss UFOlogist Erich von Shamigan came with me to see if the place was anything like how he had described it in his books. After a long day of hiking in the hot sun we came to our destination. High up in the mountains, among the sun-baked ruins of Mayan temples, is the mysterious plain of Shnazca, upon which lies some of the most intriguing markings ever seized upon by imaginative journalists.

These markings, when seen from the ground, look like nothing more than the tracks of wheelbarrows that have been pulled haphazardly across the plain by roving donkeys. Yet, when viewing them from an airplane (see figure 1A), one can see indisputable proof that the plain was the site of a gigantic game of intergalactic tic tac toe! Archaeological studies of soil samples from the plain have shown that, in all probability, X won the game (see figure 1B).

But this is not the only proof of extraterrestrial connections found on the Shnazca plain. If it were, this would be a very short chapter indeed.

A few miles to the south of these markings lies the village of Tia Manyana (literally: the place to store coca leaves). This quaint village of smiling peasants was made famous by Mr. von Shamigan in his landmark book, *Wheelbarrows of the Gods*. In his book, von Shamigan describes how he translated the petroglyphs found on stone tablets which he stole from the local science museum. The tablets describe in graphic detail how gods descended from the skies centuries ago and taught the residents

18 Flying Saucers Are Everywhere

Figure 1A

Figure 1B

Wheelbarrows of the Gods 19

of Tia Manyana how to dance the "cha-cha." After months of studying these heretofore undeciphered drawings, von Shamigen came up with the following translation:

> One, two, cha-cha-cha
> Three, four, cha-cha-cha
> Front, back, cha-cha-cha
> Turn around, cha-cha-cha.

Could it be that the ancient space travelers were preparing the locals for a huge wedding reception to be held on the Shnazca plain? Is it possible that the Ruler of the Galactic Empire was planning to be married to Princess Leia right here on our own tiny planet? Is it conceivable that Darth Vader might even have made an appearance on the plains of ancient Mexico? Probably not, but speculation like this has been known to sell quite well with cult fans, so I thought I'd throw some in.

But we're still not finished with the Mayans. If the Shnazca plains and the Tia Manyana tablets are not enough, the petroglyphs of the Cancan peninsula are a sure-fire heart stopper. For here, among the quiet lagoons off the Gulf of Mexico, is a prehistoric temple, whose walls are covered with sketches of unearthly creatures carrying laser guns (see figure 1C). These figures, drawn nearly 5,000 years ago, are ancient depictions of what can only be the triangle people from the planet Vertex!

What modern-day parent hasn't seen drawings nearly identical to this brought home from kindergarten and stuck up on the refrigerator door? Yet, how did the ancient Mayan artists know how to draw the same figures that children would be drawing several thousand years in the future? Were they inspired by space travelers who could also go forward in time?

Other temples in the area show even more proof. Within five square kilometers of the Vertex figures we can find drawings of Bloony, the banana-nosed bird man (figure 1D); Goby, the eight-legged space gator (figure 1E); and a very detailed sketch of the landing of a space traveler from the mysterious planet of the stick people (figure 1F).

20   Flying Saucers Are Everywhere

Figure 1C

*   *   *

We could go on and on about the discoveries in Central America; but then we wouldn't have time to discuss the UFOs among the ancient Egyptians, and there were plenty of UFOs flying around back in ancient Egypt. We know this because, for one thing, the pyramids are always pointing upward to the sky, leaving an unmistakable message for all ages that there are flying saucers up there.

But, as if that isn't enough, the Egyptians have left us other

Wheelbarrows of the Gods 21

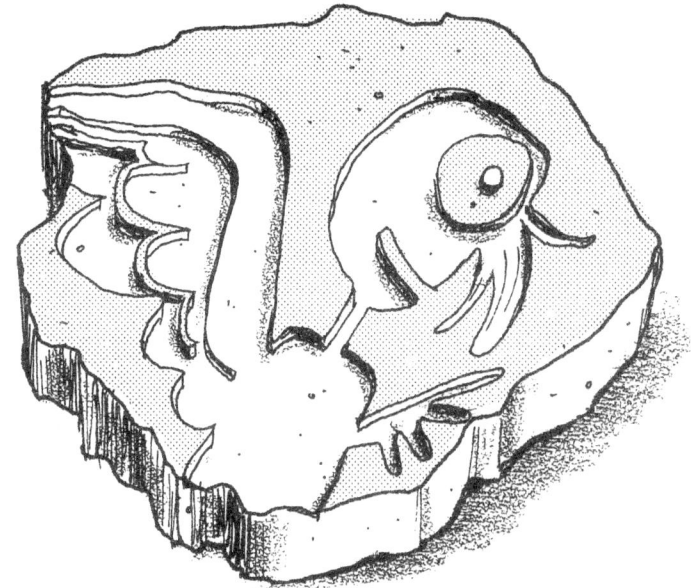

Figure 1D

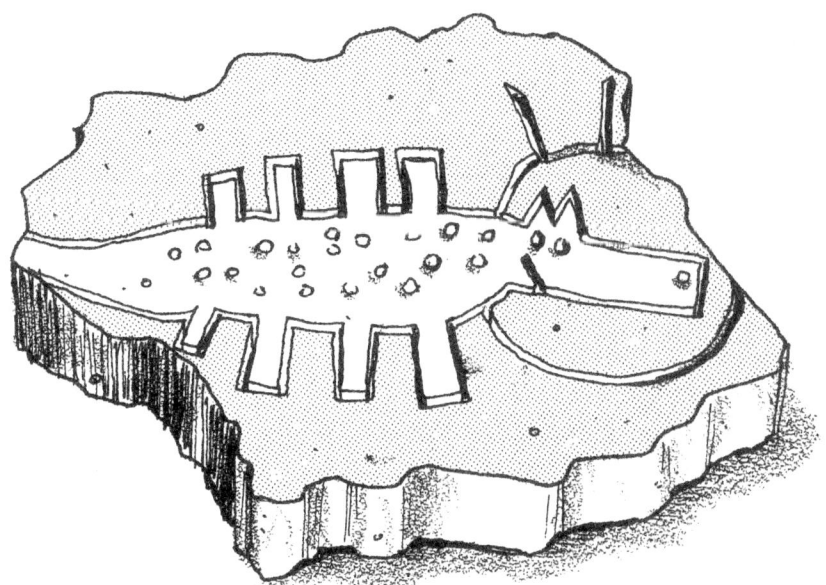

Figure 1E

signs of visitors from space. The Great Pyramid of Chutzpah, for example, is overflowing with proof that the ancient Egyptians had advanced knowledge of science and mathematics that could only have been brought to them from another planet. Consider the following facts about this prehistoric monolith and tell me there's nothing mysterious about it:

- The area of the pyramid divided by its age gives the approximate average monthly gain of the S & P 500 since 1969.

- The width of the pyramid divided by its circumference, multiplied by one billion jillion, is approximately equal to today's national debt (yet the Egyptians knew nothing about economics!).

- If a line were drawn right through the middle of the pyramid, it would pretty much divide it into two, equal half pyramids.

- If a man stands in the exact center of the pyramid, with an electronic calculator, and divides his weight by his height, the answer can be computed to many decimal places (depending on the calculator).

- If you were to stand at the very top of the pyramid on the day of the vernal equinox and face into the wind you would very likely get sand in your eyes.

- If you shave your armpits with a razor that has been kept under the great pyramid, the hair will grow back even thicker.

- If you sleep in the chambers of the great pyramid with a herd of camels, for just one night, it will take weeks to get the smell out of your clothes.

- If a man is running naked around the perimeter of the pyramid and he trips in a small hole, he is exactly twice as likely to get sand in his navel as he is to be stung by a scorpion.

- If you were standing at the entrance of the great pyramid and I were to pull your underwear up over your head, while you were still wearing it, I would be giving you a "wedgey."

Could all of these amazing facts be coincidental, or were they carefully thought up over the centuries by imaginative tour guides? Either way, they are just the tip of the iceberg of flying saucer testimony left by the ancient Egyptians. The accounts translated from the hieroglyphics are astounding.

Carved into a set of sandstone tablets recovered from the banks of the Nile river is one of the oldest examples of Egyptian hieroglyphics ever found. These tablets, known as the "Gall Stones," were first thought to be a boring record of an inventory taken by the Pharaoh Skrotumhotep I (literally: he who shuns women for camel jockeys). But modern translations of the stones have found them to reveal some of the most convincing evidence yet that Egypt was a landing base for extraterrestrial visitors.

The writings of the first tablet are shown in figure 1G. This sequence of pictures was originally translated to mean this:

> Six man slaves
> Five woman slaves
> Eight diseased quail chicks
> (By the way, did you hear what the pharaoh
> said to the snake charmer? Take my harem,
> please. Ha! Ha!)[1]
> Twenty-two horses
> Seven rabbits

---

1. Egyptian scribes had a tendency to make little jokes about the pharaohs on official documents such as inventories. They could get away with this because they were the only ones who knew how to read and write. This is why we often see silly comments about the pharaohs written on the side of the pyramid they were buried in. For example, at the entrance of one pyramid, the sign says, "Here lies Homer II, who was so ugly we had to bury him in a box of kitty litter."

24   Flying Saucers Are Everywhere

>   Ten bushels of wheat
>   Nineteen video cassettes
>   Forty-one kilograms of rocket fuel
>   Sixteen bushels of corn
>   Thirteen dilithium crystal laser guns
>   Five tons of cotton
>   etc.

Apparently a boring list of things stored in the pharaoh's warehouse. However, scholars have recently learned that, when the symbol of the woman with no arms and a beard is followed immediately by the quail chick pooping in a tea cup, it changes the meaning of the tablet from an inventory into a poem. Following this new understanding, the tablet has been retranslated into this poem about Ptooey, the Egyptian god of spit:

Figure 1F

Let us praise Ptooey
He who rules the golden spittoons
He keeps them safe and upright
So they fall not on our pantaloons
Ptooey helps us slick our hair back
And keep it there on windy days
He lets us enjoy our tobacco wads
He helps us in many ways
Ptooey, Ptooey, Ptooey
What would we do without you
Ptooey Ptooey Ptooey
We really like to sing your praise.

This new translation shows us that the Gall Stones are actually the story of a space visitor who landed in a golden rocket which impressed the Egyptians so much they built miniature models of it and used them as spittoons. Have you ever wondered why spittoons look so much like spaceships?[2]

The poem also brings up the question of how the ancient Egyptians knew about pantaloons when all they wore were towels. Clearly they must have seen a space traveler wearing them when he first came down the ladder from his cockpit.

And, finally, we have the age-old question of how tobacco was brought to Egypt from the New World in 3000 B.C. The space traveler named Ptooey must have picked up a few pouches on his way over from Mexico.

But Egypt is far from the last place where I encountered evidence of extraterrestrials. On a deserted plain in Wiltshire, England, there is a formation of megalithic stones that have brooded over the land since 2000 B.C. This circular array of towering granite was once thought to be an oversized altar for the rituals of druid priests. Yet, careful scientific studies have shown that it is actually a sundial that can predict, to within a month or so, the beginning of each polo season.

The mystery of this place, now called Stonehenge, is that

---

2. Neither have I.

26   Flying Saucers Are Everywhere

Figure 1G
Hieroglyphics from "The Gall Stones"

its ancient builders could track time more accurately than any British civilization that has followed them. Modern Englishmen are notorious at determining time as anyone who has been to a cricket match will tell you. They've been known to play the same match for days because no one can remember what time they started.

Are we to believe that such a nation built Stonehenge 4,000 years ago? Impossible! Even as late as Shakespeare's time, in 1600 A.D., the British couldn't agree on when and where the sun was coming up. Just look at this excerpt from Shakespeare's famous tragedy *The Stones upon Hengefordshire*:

> Blockheadius: Oh, sirs, doth not the sun ariseth there betwixt yon boulders?
> Bolonius: Nay, kind cretin, but here it riseth nigh upon mine sword, where the megalithic stone dost have a crack'n't.
> Insidius: Nay, I fearst thou both art dunc'd. The sun ariseth not for many an hour, as mine watch doth say 'tis only nine o'clock.
> Blockheadius and Bolonius: Oh. (*Both exeunt.*)

Certainly a civilization that couldn't even read their own watches didn't have the ingenuity to build a wonder such as Stonehenge. So who could have come up with the relatively advanced knowledge required to perform this feat?

Perhaps the answer lies across the English Channel in the famous caves of Nieuxxe de Cavarne (literally: the nasal cavities). These historic caves are known to be the dwellings of some of the earliest Homo sapiens. But who are the mysterious creatures depicted in the drawings on the walls of these caves? (See Figure 1H.) Why do they have antenna-like projections coming out of their heads? Could they be communicating with flying saucers in orbit around the earth? Perhaps they used their anti-gravity drive to move the massive boulders of Stonehenge.

The evidence can't be denied. Clues like this exist in every corner of the world. As far away as India we read about the mythical Chandrasaccharin, who floated down from the

Figure 1H

heavens on his flying cow and sprinkled a sugar substitute on the people of Krishnaramaharebrahminpunjab (literally: the land of the people with extremely long names).

In China there are the tablets of Chow On Dung, which tell the story of strange men who came to Earth in flying machines.[3] And even in North America, the Hopi Indian tribe tells the story of gods from the East who brought gifts of firewater and taught them the sacred mantra that is still proclaimed today: "Tax-Free Cigarettes, Next Exit."

Are we to believe that such legends are merely figments of primitive imaginations? Not for a moment. The evidence is too compelling, the implications are too severe, and we still have several chapters to go. In the next chapter we'll examine the scriptures that are held sacred by most of Western civilization. We will look, with our one-track mind, at the words of the Judeo-Christian prophets that have been faithfully passed down through the generations, and we will see that, even in The Bible, flying saucers are everywhere.

---

3. Unfortunately, they were all killed trying to teach the locals how to drive them.

Two

Flying Saucers in the Bible

As anyone who has studied the Bible knows, there are a great number of different translations of it. There is the King James version, the Bloody Mary version, the Cape Cod, the Tom Collins, and the Old Grandad versions, to name just a few. These were all done during the Middle Ages when it was fashionable to name your translation after your favorite drink. But, while they may be good enough for religious people, UFOlogists never pay much attention to these versions. These translations misinterpret the many references to flying saucers that were in the original scriptures, erroneously describing them as angels and cherubim.

The official UFOlogy translation of the Bible was given to Mrs. Betty-Lou Babcock by aliens from the planet Altair who visited her Kentucky home in 1954. This version, known as the Altairian Bible, contains the most accurate interpretation of the Bible's references to space visitors. Most likely, the translators of the more conventional versions were afraid they'd be labeled heretics if they printed the truth about these passages. Either that or they just couldn't read Altairian. Anyway, the Altairian translation shows that flying saucers were around even before Adam and Eve.

32 Flying Saucers Are Everywhere

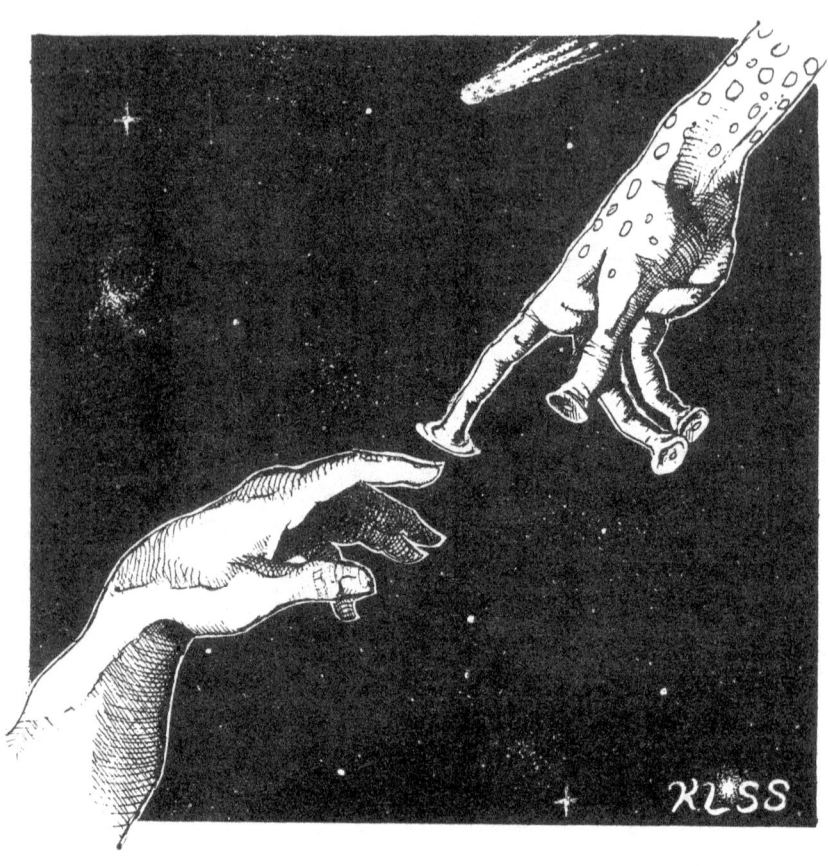

Here is the Altairian translation of chapter 1 of the Book of Genesis:

> In the beginning God created heaven and earth. And that was all God did on the first day, which was Monday, because he was in a bad mood. After all, it was his first day of work after being on vacation for most of the eternity that came before that.
> On the second day, God created great beasts such as dragons and sea monsters, including the Loch Ness monster

which can still be glimpsed to this day. He said unto them, "get thee to Bermuda or the vicinity thereof, where thou mightst prey upon ships and planes and swallow them up whole, creating mystery and intrigue for the generations."

On the third day, God created the Bigfoot, the Sasquatch and the Abominable Snowman and he distributed them to the ends of the earth so that all men might see them and repeat stories about them around the fire on camping trips.

n A d it was on the fourth day, Thursday, that God made the flying saucers. He said unto them, "be fruitful and multiply, and do ye long division and ye theory of relativity by which ye shalt travel darned near the speed of light." And then God commandeth them, "Hover ye above the earth, bring forth ye bug-eyed occupants and perpetrate ye close encounters unto the little humans, which I will make on the sixth day. Then taketh ye unto the tabloids with bizarre pictures of thy likeness." And that is why, to this day, the majority of flying saucers are seen on Thursdays, in honor of the day on which they were created.

On the fifth day, God's computer crashed and he spent all day waiting for the service engineer, so not much work got done that day.

It was on the sixth day, as promised above, that God made man and woman. God named the man Adam and he called the woman Eve, and he put fig leaves on their private parts so we could draw pictures of them in children's books.

Adam and Eve lived very happily in the Garden of Eden because it was paradise. They got two delicious shakes every day and a sensible meal at dinner time. But God's strictest rule was that Adam and Eve should never, no matter how hungry they got—they should never, *ever* eat from the Tree of Snacks Between Meals or they would surely get fat.

But, one day, the lowly serpent talked Eve into feeding Adam some french fries from the Tree of Snacks Between Meals and it was all over. God became very angry when he discovered Adam had eaten from the forbidden tree because they were the last french fries of the season. So, to punish Adam and Eve, God made them invent the wheel from scratch, which was a great hardship and took many generations.

In chapter 2 of Genesis, the Altairian Bible describes what scholars call the "begatitudes." In this chapter we learn that:
Adam begat Seth,
Seth begat Igor,
Igor begat Gilligan and
Gilligan begat Mingo.
Then, Mingo begat Gomer,
Gomer begat Goober,
Goober begat Ernie and
Ernie begat Piglet (for Ernie slept with the hogs).
Then, Piglet begat Lemmings,
Lemmings begat Charliehorse,
Charliehorse begat Pinhead and
Pinhead begat Margaret, who lived in the house that Jack built.

Finally, Jack and Margaret gave birth to a son and named him Noah.

Noah was a pivotal character in the Bi le, mainly because he had three very clumsy sons named Shem, Mo, and Larry. The flying saucer occupants, who were still called gods by earth men in those days, used to love looking down from their space ships and watching Noah's sons fighting and tripping all over each other. One day, when the gods were especially bored, they asked Noah to have his boys build an ark out of cubits. As far as we can tell, cubits were planks of wood that were used in a puzzle game invented by the prophet Rubik.

Now when the space people watched Noah's three sons trying to put all these cubits together into an ark, they were simply overwhelmed with laughter. Shem would put his cubit down on Larry's toe, then Larry would bend over and smack his cubit into Mo, who would turn around and poke Shem and Larry in the eyes with his fingers. The sight was so hilarious that the gods laughed themselves to tears. They laughed so hard, in fact, that a flood of tears covered the earth for forty days and forty nights.

Fortunately, the ark was finished before the floodwaters rose too high and Noah, his sons, and their wives were able

Flying Saucers in the Bible 35

to survive. By the time the waters subsided, however, everyone else on earth had drowned, so it was up to Shem, Mo, and Larry to continue the human race. This episode in biblical history shows us that the space visitors often took advantage of their status as gods, and that they had a rather sadistic sense of humor.

This is further demonstrated by another scene from the Bible, where space men visited Lot in his home in the city of Sodom. This time the visitors told Lot they were angels who wanted Lot's help in refinishing their lawn. (Sodom, of course, was well known for its skilled sodomites, or makers of sod.) But as soon as Lot let them into the city, they began striking people with blindness and bringing down fire and brimstone, which just ruined all that valuable sod. The "angels" allowed Lot and his family to flee the city before it was completely destroyed, but they couldn't resist turning his dog into a pillar of salt and using him to melt slugs. As a final gesture of their twisted wit, the angels forced Lot's daughters to name their children Moab and Jehosaphat.

The primitive people of Earth occasionally struck back at their heavenly tormentors and once they nearly succeeded. In the city of Babel, a clever tribe of earth men got hold of the blueprints for one of the alien rocket ships. They secretly proceeded with plans to build a rocket of their own that would put them on equal footing with the gods. To cover up their intentions, they told the gods they were building a towering temple that would reach all the way to heaven, so sacrifices could be delivered by hand instead of having to burn them all the time.

The prototype rocket was almost completed when the aliens discovered what it really was, so some secret agents were sent down to infiltrate Babel and sabotage the project. The agents told the earth men they could give them some magic words that would make their rocket even better than the rockets of the gods. They took the lead engineers aside, one at a time, and told each of them a different set of magic words, assuring each one that he was the only one who knew them. According to records found at the library of Astralbanister, one earth man was told that the magic words were:

> Peter Piper's Pagan Pals are Pompous Pigheads.

Another rocket builder was told to recite this:

> Holy Hal Hocked His Harlot to Hail a Helicopter.

Still another was told that these words would perform the task:

> She Spies Spaceships in the Spyglass.

And, finally, the last of the ambitious men from Babel was told to recite:

> Building Babel Baffles the Befuddled Babylonians.

After planting these seeds of confusion, the alien spies slipped away and left the rocket builders to wallow in chaos. When the engineers got back together, they became so confused and tongue-tied trying to get the magic words right that a war ensued and the rocket was destroyed in the cross fire. The incident at Babel delayed the development of the earth men's space program for several millennia. It also had a significant impact on the development of language.

Of all the characters in the Bible, Moses was the one who had the most contact with space aliens. The Book of Exodus tells the story of how Moses while tending his sheep on Mount Sinai, was first contacted by an alien called Yahweh. Yahweh appeared to Moses in the form of a mysterious bush that emitted fire but was not burned. The Altairian Bible tells how Moses approached this bush and attempted to roast wieners over it before it startled him and began to speak. The burning bush was most likely a radio transmitter with an exposed connection, so it gave off sparks when it came in contact with the sheep's wool. That is probably why Yahweh instructed Moses to take off his shoes, so that the smell might drive away the sheep before the radio exploded.

Later on in Exodus, Yahweh gives Moses some detailed, technical instructions on how to build the Ark of the Covenant, an instrument through which Yahweh would communicate with his people! If we follow these instructions today, using modern technology and substituting a few key words, the miraculous result is a portable color TV set. Perhaps that is how the Israelites were able to seek the advice of biblical characters like Jethro, Gomer, Festus, and Judge Wopner. We can also assume that, in their lighter moments, the Israelites entertained themselves by watching reruns of their ancestors Shem, Mo, and Larry.

The Bible is full of passages that link Moses and his followers to a space-age technology. We are told that Yahweh descended from heaven in a winged "cloud" emitting smoke and fire, that he made a loud noise, and that anyone coming near him when he was coming or going would be killed. If we simply replace the word "cloud" with "commercial airliner," we can see that Yahweh used a means of travel quite familiar to twentieth-century man. This perspective also helps to make sense of the following passage from chapter 20 of Exodus in the Altairian Bible:

> Yahweh called unto Moses from within the [commercial airliner] and commandeth him to come up to the mountain and to bringeth his priests with him. And upon the mountain he said unto them, "There shalt be no smoking and ye shalt be limited to two carry-on bags apiece, which shalt fit in the overhead compartment or under the seat in front of thee."

Once they had been taken up from the mountain, Moses was given detailed, scientific instructions on agriculture, medicine, food preparation and goat-slaughtering. For example, chapter 27 of Exodus tells of Yahweh's amazing instructions on how to prepare the daily "sacrifice," which was offered to Yahweh in his "tabernacle" every "evening":

Ye art to maketh a framework of metal, one cubit by one cubit by one and a half cubits and thou art to affix to it a molding. The molding shalt be decorated with three settings, and the settings shalt be labeled: low, medium, and high. And within the framework thou shalt affix a rotisserie of clear crystal or of a plastic substitute. . . .

Ye shalt place a leg of lamb unto a clean browning pan and it shalt be placed unto the middle of the rotisserie. Potatoes shalt be placed along the perimeter of the lamb, and thou shalt puncture the potatoes with a fork, lest they explode whilst cooking. . . .

Thou shalt cook the sacrifice for ten minutes upon the medium setting and then thou shalt cook it again for five minutes upon the high setting. Let stand for two minutes before serving. . . .

Thou shalt offer only red wine with beef and lamb and white wine shalt be offered with poultry and fish. . . .

In the book of Leviticus (literally: dungarees) Moses is given some dietary and health rules which could just as easily be taken from our own modern-day health codes:

Chooseth ye the oat bran over bacon and eggs at breakfast and thou shalt have less cholesterol and, perhaps, even find a toy surprise inside the box. . . .

And when thou goest to the chariot races, beware the pork rinds for they are abundantly fattening and wilt givest thee a wretched foulness of the breath. . . .

And always wipe ye the seat before using a public toilet lest ye catcheth the crabs or contracteth the jock itch. . . .

Moses was far from the last character in the Bible to communicate with the extraterrestrials. The Hebrew prophets who came after him showed extensive knowledge of the alien technology, especially in military matters. The aliens used the prophets as ambassadors to the earthlings and gave them special powers so they could frighten the masses into obedience. In some cases, the prophets used weapons of mass destruction that wiped out entire armies. Isaiah, for example, used a fiery cloud to defeat the army of the Aramaens, who were worshipers of a god named Baal, obviously a rival of the alien Yahweh.

The position of prophet appears, from historical records, to have been a powerful but unstable one. If a rival alien defeated the god whom a prophet worked for, the prophet would be faced with serving a new "god" or risking execution as a collaborator with the enemy. Because of this, a prophet had to be ready to switch sides at a moment's notice. The following résumé of a prophet was found among the ruins of the library of Hammurabi. Although it is considered apocryphal by the church, historians believe it may actually have been written by the biblical prophet Elijah:

Résumé of a Prophet

Name: Elijah

Address: 100 Caves of the Brotherhood Way, Sinai Desert

Objective: Position as a messenger of God or other heavenly deity in communications with earthbound humans.

Education: Studied at the University of the Prophets and received a Bachelor of Bad Tidings Degree, Class of 910 B.C.

Professional Experience: Played key role in battles between Yahweh and Baal as prophet of Yahweh during reign of King Ahab. Closely supervised such projects as raining fire from heaven, felling the walls of cities, and tormenting unfaithful kings. Extensive experience in the calling forth of droughts, the instigation of wars, and the anointing and dethroning of kings.

Hardware Experience: Have ridden in Whirlwind Model II Space Chariot and the Model G Fiery Horse Sidecar. Remote control experience with Ezekiel Winged-Cloud Hovercraft as well as the Plague-on-Your-House Aerial Crop Duster.

References: King Ahab of Israel, King Ben-hadad of Aram, Lord Yahweh of Heaven.

As we can see from this résumé, Elijah had a lot of experience flying in different types of space vehicles. In fact, Elijah eventually retired from his career as a prophet and flew to Venus on the frequent flier points he had accumulated over the years. Such were the benefits of being a prophet for the aliens.

There is much more flying saucer testimony to be found in the Bible. With the aid of modern science and an active imagination we can see how the *manna* which the Hebrews ate in the desert was actually Oreo cookies from heaven. The Altairian Bible even explains how children would peel them apart and lick the middle before dipping them in goat's milk.

A little research can also prove that Jacob's ladder was the escalator to a shopping mall, built by the aliens in an attempt to make the Middle East a major trade center. The Gate of Heaven Shopping Mall still stands today, serving earthly tourists and perhaps waiting for the return of its builders.

Even in the New Testament we can find flying saucers all over the place—from the Star of Bethlehem, which led the three wise men on their journey to Cape Canaveral, to the miracle of the loaves and the fishes, which occurred at precisely the same time as a huge Fillet o' Fish promotion by the McDonald's on Mars.

Entire books have been written on the subject of biblical UFOs, but my attention span is too short for that. We have covered enough of it here to offend the majority of religious people, so it is time to move on. In the next chapter we'll have a look at post-biblical history, and we'll discuss what they didn't tell you in school about the influence flying saucers had on the development of modern civilization.

Three

What They Didn't Tell You in History Class about Flying Saucers

On March 29, 312 A.D., the Roman emperor Constantine was riding his horse when he was startled by the sight of a glowing, saucer-shaped apparition.[1] Constantine was so affected by this sighting that he immediately issued the Edict of Mylanta, which temporarily cured all Romans of intestinal gas and heartburn. The edict also outlawed the practice of feeding Christians to the lions, a popular form of entertainment in those days. From then on only Protestants could be fed to the lions.

This is just one example of how flying saucers have influenced the development of modern civilization and provided a cure for minor ailments. Other examples can be found throughout the pages of any UFOlogy history book. Take, for example, the fall of Rome in the fourth century A.D. Few people realize the important role that flying saucers played in the decline of this great empire.

The Greek historian Commodius wrote that Attila and his

---

1. Most history books describe this apparition as a cross, but we assume that is a mistake because there are no known aliens who travel in crosses. Crosses just aren't very aerodynamic.

army of Huns were led south from Germany by a "brilliant cloud." This cloud eventually led the Huns all the way to northern Italy, where they humiliated the Romans by cornering the market on garlic and forcing them to pay a tax on it.

In the meantime, a similar cloud was leading the Vandals down the western end of the Roman Empire. Armed with nothing but rocks and spray paint, the Vandals marched all the way to Tunisia, where they established a headquarters and defaced subway cars for the next few centuries. It is likely that the aliens who assisted these barbarians had decided that the Roman Empire was becoming too modern and was better off destroyed before it invented rap music.

Alien influence also played a key role in the Crusades, during which European Christians battled Moslems from the Middle East for control of the Holy Land. The Crusades were instigated by the aliens in order to prolong the Middle Ages and postpone the beginning of the Renaissance. The aliens feared that once the Renaissance got underway, Leonardo da Vinci would invent the helicopter and they would no longer have sole control of the skies.[2] So they started a long series of destructive Holy Wars.

The first Crusade was triggered in 1095, when a UFO landed in the court of Pope Urban II, who was known for his fondness for large cities. The aliens convinced Pope Urban that the world would end unless he persuaded half of Europe to dress up in clumsy armor and march over the Alps to the Holy Land. This did not appear to be an easy task at first, so the pope sought the assistance of a folk singer named Peter the Hermit. Peter rode around the continent on his ass, singing such inspiring songs as "Hey Mister Tamerlane Man" and "Leavin' on a

---

2. When the Renaissance finally started, the aliens hypnotized Leonardo, causing him to become obsessed with a homely woman named Mona Lisa. This prevented him from actually building his helicopter, although he did draw up the blueprints for it. The noisy machine was not physically constructed until a few centuries later, after the aliens decided it may be useful in drowning out rap music.

Caravan," until people started lining up to be fitted with clumsy armor—as long as Peter promised not to go to the Holy Land with them.

At about the same time, another spaceship landed in front of the tent of the Sultan of Sinbad to warn him of the army approaching his land from the north. Clearly the aliens wanted the Moslems to win this first round. They even gave the Sultan a supply of magnetic cannon balls which couldn't miss the armored Christians, no matter how badly they were aimed.

But, in order to ensure a stalemate, the aliens fixed the next round of Crusades in favor of the Christians. An "angel" visited Sir Godfrey of Bouillon and presented him with a powerful laser gun that he was supposed to use against the heathen Moslems. Instead, Sir Godfrey used it to freeze-dry his soup into little cubes which he tried to market as a practical new field ration. The trend didn't catch on right away and Sir Godfrey was thrown into an asylum; but the Christians won anyway by hurling their armor at the Moslems, causing their magnetic cannon balls to boomerang back on them. Thus the Crusades raged back and forth for over 150 years before word got around that Peter the Hermit was dead and that it was safe to return to Europe.

After the Crusades, the Europeans spent the next few centuries building cathedrals and decorating them with pictures of the aliens. Almost every painting drawn in the Middle Ages depicts heavenly beings with halos around their heads, indicating that they wore space helmets, much like the astronauts of our own time. Heavenly beings in these paintings are also surrounded by naked babies with wings, but that was probably just an artistic custom of the time (see figure 3A).

In the 1500s, on January 13th, at about three in the afternoon, Paris time, the Renaissance finally began. It was triggered by the birth of the French astrologer Nostradamus, who, even as an infant, had quite a knack for predicting the future. His mother said that he would consistently wrinkle up his nose just moments before a major poop would occur. But, once he got older, Nostradamus became famous for predicting far into the future by reading *quatrains* (Latin for horse droppings).

Figure 3A
A Typical Middle Ages Painting

Nostradamus claimed that his gift of prophecy was given to him by *beings* from a *higher plane*. "Higher than what?" he was often asked. "How should I know?" he would reply, "I don't even know what a plane is? All I know for sure is that *beings* is supposed to be italicized." But we can assume that the UFOs were responsible for his foresight, because it's as good an explanation as any. Here are some of Nostradamus' predictions that have already come true:

A man will be born of simple origins
And sing and dance 'til he's accused of sins.
But, after selling a billion disks of bop,
His home will be toured for twenty bucks a pop.
(Elvis Presley sells one billion records and his home becomes a profitable museum.)

The faction named for the municipality
Will, from behind, take Eastern seniority,
And, after falling once to the orange and black,
Will stage a rally and all the way come back.
(NY Mets defeat Baltimore four games to one in the 1969 World Series.)

The maker of foods of grease will come around
And market a burger of a leaner ground.
Then clients will be offered, for dessert,
A cone of lowfat frozen yogurt.
(McDonald's begins selling fast foods that are lower in fat.)

A vexed family drawn from foreign ink
Will lead the minds of children down the sink
The adolescent hero spreads his dirt
By sending forth his image on a shirt.
(The controversial cartoon "The Simpsons" becomes a worldwide sensation among young people and Bart Simpson T-shirts create a furor in schools.)

One of the most obvious proofs that flying saucers were still around during the Renaissance is the world-famous Piri Reis map. Piri Reis, an admiral in the Turkish navy, was the most skilled map maker of the seventeenth century. A sample of one of his maps, shown in figure 3B, was found at the library of Alexandria and displayed in museums for centuries as a curiosity, but no one could figure out what land masses it was supposed to portray.

Then in 1940, researchers discovered a larger, more comprehensive map, of which the first was just a subset (see figure 3C). This larger map put Piri Reis' cartography methods into a much better perspective. It showed that the admiral understood the importance of the Areola Borealis centuries before it was rediscovered by Masters and Johnson in the 1960s.

By the time the Renaissance came to an end, the seeds of revolution had been planted in France, and some of those seeds were of extraterrestrial origin. As early as the reign of Louis XV, "the saucer king," the royal palace was visited by strangers whose clothes looked peculiar to the fashion-conscious French. One palace guard of the era wrote in his diary:

> The strangers with the short hair visited the king again today. They showed up at the palace entrance wearing tight-fitting costumes and carrying a bottle filled with a mysterious orange liquid. They told the king that this liquid was most tasteful when poured lightly over a garden salad and asked if they could trade it for a bottle of champagne, which they wanted to use to christen their newest airship.

Later, during the reign of Louis XVI, aliens were commonly seen conspiring with Queen Marie Antoinette. This may explain why the queen, when warned that her subjects were starving, would often blurt out, "Let them eat Moon Pies!"

At the same time, the aliens were cultivating a relationship with the man who was to become the most notorious conqueror of Europe: Napoleon Bonaparte. While growing up on Corsica, the young Bonaparte used to brag to his classmates that he was visited by "comrades from heaven," who told him he would grow up to be a famous epileptic.

What They Didn't Tell You in History Class   49

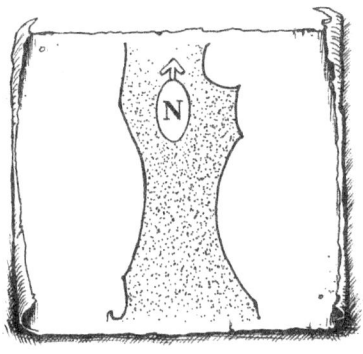

Figure 3B

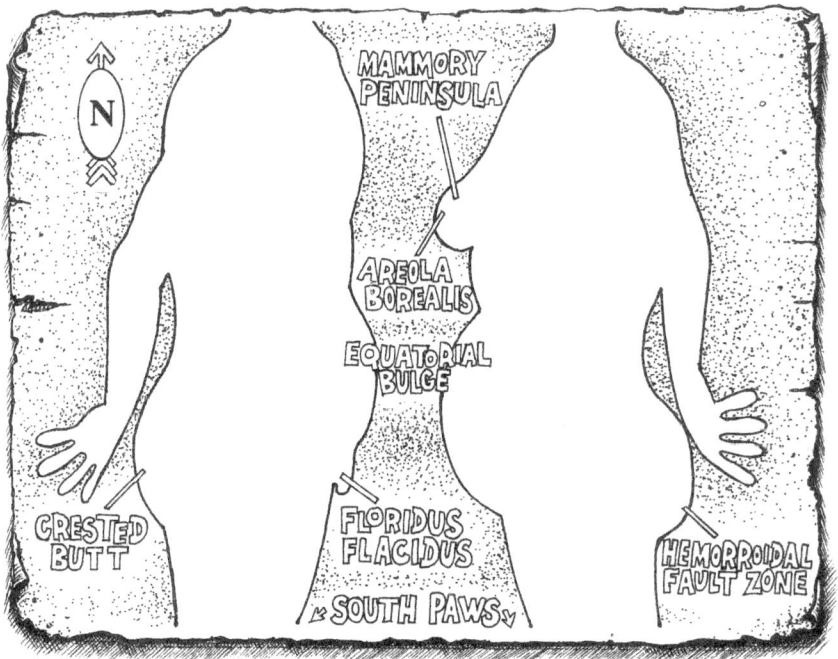

Figure 3C

After he became a general, there were rumors that a light-skinned foreigner would visit Napoleon to discuss military fashion issues. This foreigner is believed to have influenced Napoleon's selection of the numerous hat designs that he used throughout his reign. As the reader can see in figure 3D, many of these designs look suspiciously advanced for the early 1800s.

Sightings of UFOs and aliens continued all through the nineteenth century and into the twentieth. There are well-documented rumors that the space visitors maintained contact with the most influential people on Earth. Thomas Jefferson, for example, designed his home, Monticello, after the shape of a spacecraft which he flew in during consultations with extraterrestrials. Honest Abe Lincoln used to tell friends that he had a special advisor who came to him from another planet. Everyone assumed he was talking about General Grant, but it may well have been an alien. And it wasn't just the good guys who had contacts with the space men. Adolf Hitler had connections with at least two different groups of aliens.

Hitler's experiences with the saucer people started when he was an art student at the Universität Nincompoopen. A horrified Adolf was abducted by a spaceship while trying to paint a nude portrait of himself in the Black Forest. The aliens examined the young führer and plucked samples of hair from the sides of his mustache. Due to the radiation he was exposed to, the hair never grew back and Hitler was left with the silliest-looking mustache in history, which made him a very angry man.

The Nazi leader's next encounter with aliens was in 1923 during the famous Beer Hall Putsch. In this incident, Hitler and his followers got into an argument with the patrons of a Munich pub over whether Aryan hops were better than the Semitic varieties. Just as the argument came to a head, a flying saucer appeared outside the bar to announce that the Aryan hops were less filling but that the Semitic ones tasted great.

Hitler and his fellow Nazis declared war on the saucer and chased it all over the city. The spacecraft hovered just ahead

What They Didn't Tell You in History Class

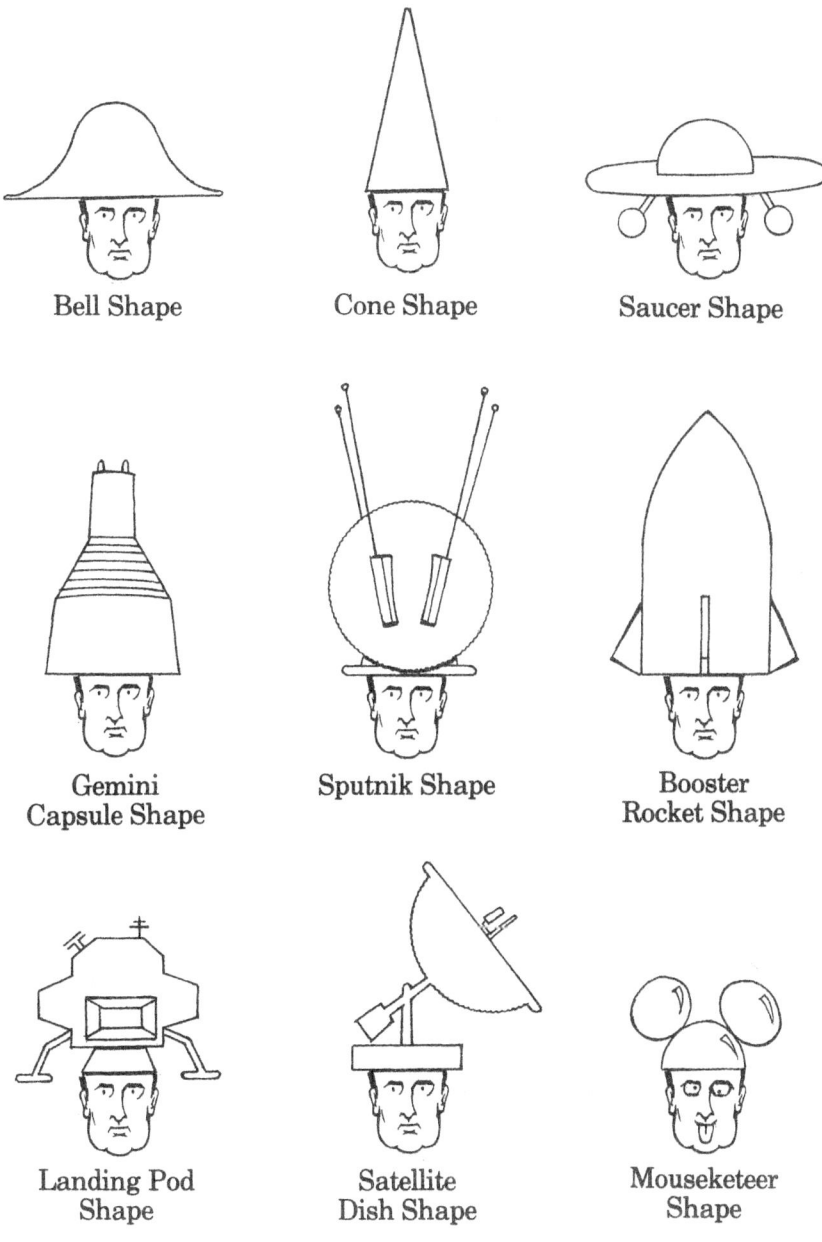

Figure 3D
Napoleon's Hat Designs

of the mob and teased them a while, then flew away before the authorities showed up. Of course, no one believed the story. It was assumed that the men with the toothbrush mustaches were part of some drug-crazed cult, so they were all thrown in jail for six months and then appointed to high government positions.

As Chancellor, Hitler made a pact with some rival aliens of the ones who had tormented him. In exchange for some of their rocket technology, Germany gave the aliens the design for the Volkswagen Beetle. The space men modified the beetle for flight, producing the famous "buggy" UFOs, which can still be seen today.

Fortunately for history, the Allies obtained the assistance of some "good guy" aliens and were able to develop microwave ovens. This led to the discovery of creative new ways of killing cockroaches, which, in turn, inspired the invention of the atomic bomb. Thus, the flying saucers brought about the end of World War II and ushered us into the age of modern UFOlogy.

So, as we can see, flying saucers have been with us from the beginning of time all the way up to the present day. It has only been in recent years, however, that mankind has recognized these UFOs for what they are. In the past few decades, we have achieved a level of technology that allows us to make a realistic, scientific examination of the phenomenon. That technology, of course, is the ability to broadcast "Star Trek" into our homes six times each day. In the coming chapters, we will carry out a careful, scientific investigation of what flying saucers really mean to mankind and how we can exploit this phenomenon to our greatest profit.

Four

Modern UFO Sightings and Close Encounters in Hickstown

Any scientific study of flying saucers should include an erroneous quote from a famous scientist. In 1949, at a UFO symposium, Dr. Albert Einstein told a captive audience of saucer fanatics, "I have always believed that the flying saucer phenomenon is totally erroneous."

Now let's get on with our study.

According to a recent poll, more than 90,000 people saw an array of dazzling lights streaking across the Los Angeles sky one night in 1990. That's enough people to fill the Los Angeles Coliseum. In fact, those people *were* in the Los Angeles Coliseum; the poll was taken at a rock concert where elaborate fireworks were used.

But it could just as well have been people from all across America, based on data provided to me by DORFS (Diligent Organization for the Research of Flying Saucers). DORFS is an organization of greasy-haired people who wear unstylish clothing and collect obscure statistics about flying saucers. Their records show that over 25 million Americans have seen an Unidentified Flying Object of one kind or another.

Modern UFO Sightings and Close Encounters

Forty-five percent of these witnesses described what they saw as a "saucer-shaped" or "disk-shaped" object. Twenty-five percent described seeing a "cigar-shaped" or "oval" aircraft. And 0.4 percent claimed they saw what looked like "a gnarly light show, dude." Again, that last 0.4 percent were in the L.A. Coliseum.

In another DORFS poll, a random sampling of Americans were asked a number of questions about flying saucers. Eighteen percent of those surveyed said they had seen a flying saucer at some time in their lives. Of those, 25 percent said they had witnessed the landing of an alien spaceship and had seen humanoid creatures inside it. Eight percent claimed they had been abducted by the aliens and were programmed to be one of the "Star People." And almost all those abducted said the aliens had given them Reece's Pieces and encouraged them to phone home.

The poll also showed that a lot of people have misgivings about the things they have seen in the sky: Twenty-one percent of those polled said they had mistaken a hot air balloon for a flying saucer. Fourteen percent said they had mistaken a flying saucer for a shooting star. Fifteen percent said they had mistaken a shooting star for a bottle rocket. And 19 percent said they had been drinking shooters from a hot water bottle.

One of the more interesting results of the DORFS poll was the question about "swamp gas" sightings. Swamp gas is a luminous gas often seen hovering over swamps at night. It is a purely natural phenomenon that is commonly mistaken for a flying saucer. Twelve percent of those who had reported a sighting said they may have mistaken swamp gas for a flying saucer. Ten percent said they had mistaken a flying saucer for a commercial airliner. Seven percent said they had mistaken a commercial airliner for swamp gas. And 19 percent said they had passed gas in a commercial swamp.

Finally, the poll participants were asked if they had ever witnessed a falling star, and if they thought falling stars might be an explanation for many UFO reports. Twenty-two percent reported they thought most UFOs were actually falling stars.

Twenty-five percent said they thought UFOs were falling aliens. Thirty-three percent said they had made a wish on a falling star. And 45 percent said they wished they could "make it" with *Aliens* star Sigourney Weaver.

In a search for scientific ways to classify UFO sightings, filmmaker Steven Spielberg came up with a method that is based on the observations of a passionate couple in different stages of lovemaking. Spielberg called these sightings *Close Encounters* and divided them into four categories:

- A **Close Encounter of the First Kind** is defined as a UFO sighting by a man and a woman while they are kissing in a remote, wooded area. Sixty-seven percent of all UFO sightings fall into this category.

- A **Close Encounter of the Second Kind** is when the UFO is sighted by a couple engaged in light foreplay. Twelve and a half percent of all sightings fall into this category.

- A **Close Encounter of the Third Kind** is when a UFO sighting causes the lovers to become obsessed with a mountain of mashed potatoes. This category accounts for about 2 percent of all sightings and can be quite messy.

- The final category, a **Close Encounter of the Fourth Kind,** is when a UFO is not seen by the passionate couple at all; or if it is, the couple doesn't care. It is impossible to determine how many sightings of this type occur, but these are said to be the most inspiring.

There are occasions when a UFO is seen by someone other than a passionate couple. Such sightings often involve sober, trustworthy citizens who may have been watching too much television. Take, for example, the case of Mrs. Thelma-Lou Bittington of Bumbling Bluff, Arkansas. On the evening of January 23, 1964, Mrs. Bittington was driving home from choir practice when she noticed what looked like a large, glowing grapefruit following her car. "I was feeling quite sober and

Modern UFO Sightings and Close Encounters 57

trustworthy that night," she later explained, "until I saw the object in my rearview mirror. It looked far bigger than any fruit I had ever seen, and it kept getting bigger, which really scared me because I have a severe allergy to citrus."

Mrs. Bittington became so startled she drove off the side of the road into a ditch before she realized the object was only a yellow balloon. It had been attached to her bumper as a promotional gimmick at the service station where she had refueled.

Mrs. Bittington was too embarrassed to tell her husband she had been frightened by a balloon, so she removed it from her bumper and let it float off into the sky where several residents of the greater Bumbling Bluff area saw it and called the newspaper. This helped substantiate Mrs. Bittington's claim when she told her husband that the damage to their car had been caused by a saucer from outer space. This incident, though it technically did not involve an actual spacecraft, triggered the great UFO "flap"[1] of 1964.

But not all UFO sightings are caused by helium balloons. In fact, balloons can account only for about 78 percent of known sightings. Other causes range from airplanes to meteorites to flashlights hanging from kite strings. The last is a technique mastered by only a few UFOlogists, but it is quite effective and very difficult to debunk (unless of course the kite is discovered, but that rarely happens). I have personally published three best-selling UFO books, under another name, that were based on a flashlight attached to a cardboard model and hung from a kite on a dark night.

Of course, some UFO sightings are more than just optical illusions. In a study conducted by myself and some other UFOlogists, where we drew some cards from a deck, it was estimated

---

1. A "flap," by the way, is a term used by UFOlogists to describe a situation where many sightings occur in the same geographic area over a short period of time. UFO flaps are of great interest to researchers like myself because they spur media attention and give us a chance to appear on "Geraldo" and "Donahue."

that the fraction of all UFOs that are genuine spaceships from other planets is somewhere between seven and jack percent. The incident described in the following newspaper story is believed to be one of these:

> CRANKSTER, MONTANA: A number of local residents reported seeing a fast-moving, unidentified vehicle in the skies around Crankster last Thursday, and at least one witness claims he saw humanoid occupants inside. Mr. Herbert Wedlow, a resident of the Garden Grove nursing home, said he saw a bright light in the sky around 7:30 P.M. He said the light hovered for a few minutes and then swooped down toward his bedroom window, coming close enough for him to see that it was a glowing spaceship with a transparent dome on top. Inside the spaceship, Wedlow said he saw two humanoid occupants sitting at a control panel and operating an instrument that looked very much like his suppository applicator.

The Wedlow case is just one of thousands of UFO sightings involving someone with a hemorrhoid condition, and it suggests that some aliens might also suffer from such discomforts.

Mr. Wedlow's experience also has some similarities to the story of Patrolman Dave Bamford from Beamington, Arizona. On June 12, 1969 at 5:45 P.M., Patrolman Bamford was burning an illegal marijuana crop, just off Highway 23, when he noticed a bright light shining a few miles up the road. Thinking that it might be an ice cream truck, Bamford fumbled for his keys and drove up the road in a zigzag fashion, since his arms were starting to feel rather heavy. Once he got close enough, Bamford noticed that the glowing object was not an ice cream truck after all, but was "shaped like a deep-dish pizza with a dome on top." Since the object was a few hundred yards off the road in a corn field, Bamford called for help and then got out of his car to have a closer look.

As he walked into the field, Bamford noticed two small, humanoid creatures playing leapfrog just outside the object. He said the little men were about four feet high, and wore helmets

Modern UFO Sightings and Close Encounters 59

and earrings, so he assumed they must be from California. When the creatures noticed Bamford for the first time, they appeared very embarrassed to find that they weren't alone. One of the humanoids made an obscene gesture with its middle finger and then they both jumped back into the spacecraft through a square door. The craft made a loud whirring noise and shot straight up into the air until Bamford lost sight of it.

Officer Michael Shamus would have seen the object, too, if he had not been detained by a particularly seductive hitchhiker on the way to answer Bamford's call. As it was, Shamus got to the scene just after the spaceship took off. He found Bamford sitting in the middle of the field, eating corn and complaining that he was famished. Bamford then showed Shamus the landing imprints left by the vehicle, which Shamus said resembled women's breasts, though Bamford insisted they were shaped more like jelly-filled donuts.

There are plenty of other instances where UFOs have left imprints in the ground. Sometimes they leave even more evidence behind. A case in point is the story of George and Mimi Redbait of Hickstown, Nebraska. On a warm July night in 1968, the Redbaits were just going to bed when they were startled by a loud bang and a brilliant flash of light. Mr. Redbait loaded his shotgun and asked his wife to stay inside while he went out to investigate.

George was heading in the direction from which the flash had come when he was startled by a small humanoid figure in a space suit. "It was about four feet high and had big ol' eyes," he later recalled. "It kind of reminded me of this guy we used to make fun of in high school, we called him grasshopper. I went to aim my gun and shoot at it but it put its little hands up as if it was surrenderin'," he continued. "So I felt sorry for it and decided not to shoot.

"Then I put the gun down and tried to communicate with it and the little thing jumped up and kicked me in the groin so hard I thought I was gonna die." George says he fell back on the ground and struggled to get his gun, but by the time he looked up again it had run off into his alfalfa field and entered an oval spaceship. He then saw the spaceship take off "faster than any plane I ever seen."

By that time, Mrs. Redbait had joined her husband in the yard with a flashlight, so the two of them went out to inspect the area where the spaceship had been. George explained to me what they found there when I interviewed him a few days later:

> All the alfalfa in the area was flattened. It wasn't burned or nothin', it was jest flattened, like somethin' heavy been lyin' on it. Then, right in the middle, was this strange, yellow colored ooze, like the stuff you cough up when you git a bad cold, if ya know what I mean.
>
> Mimi got an idea and ran inside to get a jar to collect the ooze in so she could give it to the grandchildren to play with. Meantime I went around and checked up on all the animals to make sure they was okay.

George told me that none of his animals appeared to be harmed but that his chickens were acting unusually aggressive. For the next few days, in fact, George's chickens were seen terrorizing the larger animals by flapping their wings at them and squawking loudly. The bizarre behavior finally stopped after one of his pigs grew tired of the harassment and bit one of the chicken's heads off. "After that," said George, "things pretty much settled down to normal."

The yellow ooze that the Redbaits found was taken to the local health office for examination. Researchers there identified it as a rare form of fungus that is sometimes excreted by psychotic birds and people who look like grasshoppers. They suggested that Mr. Redbait mix it with egg white and try using it as a wallpaper paste.

The Redbait sighting contains many traits that are quite common among UFO landings: short humanoids, flattened grass, yellow ooze and, again, it all occurred in a place with a silly name like Hickstown. These common traits could all be instrumental clues in solving the UFO enigma. Or they could be material for a bizarre, new TV sitcom. Either way, they bring us to a topic that has become the latest rage among UFO buffs and crackpots of all persuasions: the mysterious crop circles of Wiltshire, England.

Five

Those Mysterious Crop Circles

Wiltshire County, England, is a clean, fertile land of rolling green hills and fresh country air. The earth here has been plowed, planted, and reaped by the native farmers since the time of King Arthur. Walking through a field in this idyllic countryside, as I did last summer, I could smell the freshness of the wind brushing against my face, I could hear the crunch of delicate wheat bending beneath my feet, and I could feel the cold barrel of a shotgun poking my ribs after a farmer discovered me trampling his crops.

It was an embarrassing, not to mention dangerous, moment, but I finally bribed my way out of it by explaining to the farmer that I was lost and would be happy to pay him for directing me to the nearest crop circle formation. "Crop circle?" the farmer grunted in his Wiltshire accent. "Well, why didn't you say so?" He pointed down the road to a mile-long line of tourists. "The line forms at the rear, bloke. For *paying* customers, that is."

Why would people line up for miles and pay a pound apiece to see flattened circles of grain in an otherwise normal wheat field? Apparently because the farmer of said field has a shotgun for anyone who *doesn't* pay. How was I to know?

I had become interested in the crop circles after reading

about them in UFO journals in America. The circles began to make news in the late 1980s, when hundreds of farmers claimed they woke up in the morning to find giant circles pressed into their grain fields by some unknown force. The first reports of crop circles were simple, flattened areas that looked much like the *saucer nests* common in UFOlogy. These are areas of flattened grass found at the landing site of a UFO, presumably formed by the weight of the vehicle. Since the early crop circles were so similar, many saucer enthusiasts showed up to see what could be found in these English grain fields. In the last few years, the circles have been examined by geiger counters, dowsing rods, spirit channelers, and hunting dogs, but no one has offered a satisfactory explanation for their appearance.

As a UFO investigator, my primary interests were (1) to see if these circles were alien landing sites and (2) to get a neat trip that would be tax-deductible. So the day I arrived in Wiltshire County, I asked the tourists bureau where I could go to find the most recent crop formations. They directed me to this farmer's field in the quaint, rustic town of Headcheese-upon-Turkey-Gristle.

As I waited in the long line I made the acquaintance of other researchers and learned a few things about this puzzling phenomenon. Mr. Arthur Binghamton, a native of Wiltshire County, told me he had been investigating the subject for the last five years, since reports of the circles first started making their way around the county pubs. Mr. Binghamton was a founding member of the Center for Crop Circle Research and Ponderance (CCCRAP), an organization dedicated to studying this enigma and to downing a lot of stout in the process.

Binghamton informed me that, although the earlier formations were plain, flat circles, in later years, as the impressions increased in number, they also became more elaborate. Most of the more recent formations contained markings inside the circles or appendages branching out from the perimeter. Figure 5A shows the many shapes that have been recorded by CCCRAP. They range from the simple "doughnut" shape to the curious "cluster" formations that almost seem to be a message of some sort.

Those Mysterious Crop Circles 65

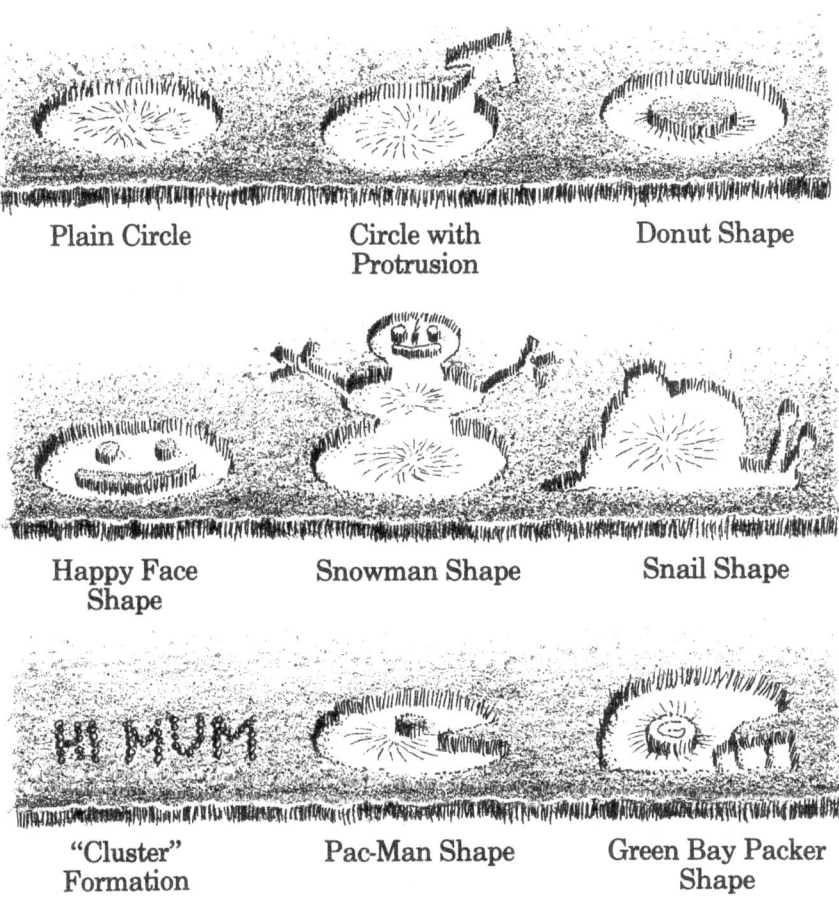

Figure 5A
Crop Circle Formations

As we waited, Mr. Binghamton filled me in on the work of CCCRAP and some of the theories they had come up with concerning the force behind the formations. One theory holds that the circles are formed by a force emanating from the nearby boulders of Stonehenge. The natives of Wiltshire have long believed that the rocks at Stonehenge possess supernatural powers that can affect the weather, ward off evil, and protect tax offenders from the exchequer. Some believe that the mysterious forces behind Stonehenge may be creating the circles as a form of communication, perhaps to warn the locals of an impending onslaught of Tolkien fanatics.

Other theories are as varied as the land is fertile. Some say the formations could be the greens of an interdimensional golf course, but since no holes or flags are ever found in the circles, that theory isn't given much credence. Another theory, favored by fans of English folklore, is that the circles are built by the *little people* for "grasshopper rodeos." These are festive occasions where elves and hobbits try to lasso grasshoppers and wrestle them off the grain onto the ground. This might explain why the grain is usually bent instead of broken.

Still another hypothesis is that the circles are formed when moths are directed into a holding pattern by their air traffic controllers, before they are brought in for a landing in the grain fields. This might explain the appendages that sometimes extend out from the circles—they could be the moths' runways. The problem with this theory is that no moths have actually been seen flying in a holding pattern and no one's ever heard of them being directed by air traffic controllers. They're only stupid little bugs, after all.

More mundane theories put forth to explain the circles include a subliminal advertising campaign, allegedly sponsored by the makers of Lifesavers, and a chemical found in the urine of hedgehogs, which might cause the grain to lie flat. Oddly enough, the hedgehog theory agrees with what some say is the fulfillment of a prophecy in a song by the former rock group Led Zepplin.

One line in Led Zepplin's classic song "Stairway to Heaven"

says: "If there's a bustle in your hedgerow, don't be alarmed now. Its just a sprinkling for the May queen." Zepplin cultists have interpreted this to mean that when one hears a bustle (a rustling noise) in one's hedgerow (a row of crops), then it is probably the hedgehogs urinating in a crop circle. This prophecy proves, among other things, that Led Zepplin fans did far too many drugs during the seventies.

But what about the flying saucers? Is there any evidence connecting these crop circles to the UFO phenomenon? I'm glad I asked. Mr. Binghamton told me that the appearance of crop circles in the morning is quite often preceded by reports of strange lights in the skies the night before. Basically, as you may have gathered, there's a crop circle theory for everyone, and if there's not one for you, feel free to make one up.

After waiting an hour or so we finally got our chance to explore the farmer's crop circles up close. A farmhand guided us through the field along the tram lines used when watering the crops and spraying them for bugs. The tram lines, we were told, were the best way to get around a field without damaging any of the crop. Oddly enough, almost all crop circles are clustered around these tram lines.

After a few minutes' walk, we came upon a large, cleared area where the grains of wheat were all laid flat, pointing outward from the center. The farmhand informed us that this was one of two circle formations that had appeared overnight. We were encouraged to examine the flattened grains of wheat and to drop money into the center of the circle while we made a wish.

As we fumbled about the circle, a dowser announced to the group that he was going to use what appeared to be a straightened coat hanger to detect forces of earth energy inside the circle. Everyone watched in silence as the dowser closed his eyes and allowed the energy to pull him around with his homemade divining rod. The man appeared to be pulled by his coat hanger over the flattened wheat along a path that took him around the entire perimeter of our wheat circle. He then leaned toward a clearing through the tram line and followed it to a second, larger circle, adjacent to the first one.

Here, the dowser stopped for a moment in quiet meditation. He then jerked toward the perimeter of the second circle, again following the edge all the way around until, suddenly, he broke the stillness with a loud, exasperated scream. We all watched in anticipation to see what the man may have found that was so terrifying. The dowser opened his eyes, looked down at his feet, and began cursing like a British sailor over those ungodly hedgehogs as he scraped dung off his boots with the end of his coat hanger.

After this inspiring experience with circle-dowsing, I asked the farmhand if I could wander into a part of the field where the grain was still standing. Since I promised not to disturb any wheat, the farmhand agreed. I carefully made my way through some tall stalks of wheat followed by Mr. Binghamton and a handful of others. Since my intention was to have a moment of privacy with nature, the company was somewhat annoying, but I was able to get a small amount of relief by passing gas among the anonymity of the stalks. Then suddenly, to my surprise, every stem of grain within twenty meters wilted to the ground, forming a spoke-like pattern all around me. Not only was all the wheat laid level but all the people within the circle were prostrate as well.

I was too embarrassed to tell them what had happened when they regained consciousness, so I pretended to be just as mystified as everyone else. The farmhand looked terrified and ran off to get the farmer, who tried in vain to charge us all an extra pound for witnessing this wonder. Tourists began pouring into the newly formed circle to investigate it and to speculate on the pungent odor associated with it. Soon the dowser was headed for my new circle, this time using a small shovel for a divining rod.

I made my way back through the tramline to the first circle and, this time, had no problem finding the privacy to relieve myself. Then, as I pondered the implications of what had just occurred, I decided I wasn't quite ready to conclude that all crop circles were formed this way. The experience did, however, enlighten me as to why the British refer to their spicy little sausages as "bangers," and I made a mental note not to eat any more of them.

Before giving up on the crop circle mystery, I drove up to Oxford to investigate a UFO sighting that may have been related to the circles. A report in a newspaper I had read described a "bevy of flying saucers" that were sighted in the skies just south of Oxford the evening before the Headcheese formations had appeared. The article said the saucers had been witnessed by dozens of trustworthy citizens, including some police officers and a professor from Oxford University.

I managed to track down the professor, Dr. Milton Dooright, when I visited the university campus. Dr. Dooright confirmed that he had seen the saucers but he said the description in the newspaper was horribly flawed. "It should never be called a *bevy* of flying saucers," he informed me, "the proper phrase is a *gaggle* of flying saucers." The professor added that to call it a "bevy of UFOs" would have been okay.

When I left Oxford, I returned to Headcheese to visit the headquarters of CCCRAP. The friendly people at CCCRAP offered me a pint of stout and showed me around their extensive crop circle museum, which included a display on the circles and related phenomena from around the world. There were pictures of formations that had appeared in mainland Europe and Australia and also a fascinating display on the "Swiss holes."

This is a phenomenon similar to the crop circles that occurs in Switzerland. Deep, circular holes are found in the rocky foothills of the Alps with no sign of how or why they were dug. The Swiss holes also attract tourists and dowsers along with endless theories about their origin. These theories range from alien laser instruments to burrowing "rock fairies" to rock-eating insects. Personally, I think they're caused by the same force that's been putting holes in their cheese for all these centuries. The folks at CCCRAP said they hadn't even thought of that.

* * *

But enough about the British circles and the Swiss holes. What about right in our own backyards? Can't we find some mystery circles here in the U.S.A.? Well of course we can. As long as we make them ourselves, that is. CCCRAP sells do-it-yourself crop circle kits by mail. The kits come complete with instructions on how to create different patterns of crop formations and even explains which ones work best on which crops. Finally, the kit tells how to attract tourists and what kind of stout to serve in your circle. To get your own crop circle kit, send 40 (forty) U.S. dollars or 25 (twenty-five) pounds sterling to:

> The Center for Crop Circle Research and Ponderance
> Post Box HOAX-12
> Headcheese-upon-Turkey-Gristle
> Wiltshire County, England

Crop circle kits have been selling swiftly in this country and many buyers have already mastered the technique. According to newspaper reports, over fifty of the mysterious circles have appeared in the Midwestern states so far this year and the forecast for next year is even more bullish.

Six

Abduction by the Aliens: The Bumpkin Story

The most fascinating, most horrifying, and most profitable aspect of the UFO phenomenon is the abduction experience. This is when innocent, unsuspecting earth people are suddenly abducted by a UFO and examined by aliens who are as intellectually superior to us as we are to, say, dogs. The abductees have provided us with the best clues yet as to the aliens' purpose for their visits to Earth and their monitoring of the human race. They have also provided us with numerous bestselling books and some *very* bad movies.

Imagine what it would be like to be your dog when he is taken to the vet for a checkup. You are brought in on a leash, crawling on four legs, covered with fur, and unable to speak. You see the vet dressed all in white, carrying sharp, pointed instruments and restraining you so you can't struggle away. He examines you, pokes you with needles, perhaps forces pills down your throat, and holds your snout shut while you're forced to swallow them. Finally, when it's all over, you're brought home in the back of the car, feeling hurt and confused. And when you get there, you are still forbidden to jump up on the couch.

This is how some UFO contactees feel after they've been abducted by the aliens. They tell of seeing a huge, brightly lit spacecraft land in front of them. Then, to their horror, they find themselves covered with fur and being dragged on a leash into the spaceship, where a muzzle is put over their snout and they are examined by creatures of a much higher intelligence. Some report that the aliens attempt to comfort them slightly by scratching them behind the ears but, overall, it's a horrifying experience.

When it's all over, the victims are brought back to the place they were abducted from, and left there with no memory of what happened. They come back to consciousness with a feeling of extreme confusion about why they are driving with their head out the window and their tongue hanging down. Some have even reported coughing up hair balls without having any clue about what has happened to them. It is only under hypnosis that the abductees are able to recall their experience with the aliens and to write bestselling books about it.

The best-documented story of a UFO abduction, at least in modern times, is the case of Betty and Barney Bumpkin of Cowpyle, New Hampshire. It was September of 1961 and the Bumpkins were returning from a vacation in Canada with their pet wiener dog, Poopsey. Mrs. Bumpkin suspected something was wrong when Poopsey began whining and pointing to the sky. "At first we couldn't see anything unusual," Betty said later; "but then, when we stopped the car, Barney and I noticed this very bright star that appeared to be moving toward us."

The Bumpkins got back in their car and quickly drove off, but the "star" stayed with them no matter how fast Barney drove. Betty said Poopsey began tracking the star with some binoculars they had in the back seat. The dog became so frightened by what she saw that she started whimpering and slithered to the floor of the car. When Betty looked through the binoculars, she noticed that the object was not a star at all. It was an aircraft in the shape of a very large hot dog bun. "No wonder poor Poopsey was so upset," she thought. As it came closer, Betty could make out six humanoid figures through a window in the odd-shaped craft. By then Poopsey was hiding under Betty's seat, and pawing some rosary beads (the Bumpkins were devout Catholics).

At this point the Bumpkins lost track of what was happening. For three years they had no memory of what had occurred between the time they saw the humanoids and the time they arrived back in their hometown of Cowpyle. "The next thing I remembered, after looking through the binoculars," Betty said, "was seeing Poopsey finishing up the rosary. I knew a lot of time must have passed because it always took her hours to get through a rosary. But, for the life of me, I couldn't remember what had happened during those hours."

For years afterward, however, the Bumpkins were plagued with bad dreams and nagging anxieties about the missing time. Finally, they decided they had to get to the bottom of this mystery, so they contacted a UFO club, the Society for Aerial Phenomenon Scrutiny, or SAPS.

The Bumpkins weren't the least bit interested in money or publicity when they went to SAPS, but they did ask, just out of curiosity, how much cash might be involved if they went public with their experience. Researchers at SAPS told them that UFO books were very hot, and the more bizarre their story was, the better it would sell. SAPS referred the Bumpkins to Dr. Hans Kopfkrummer, a former Nazi researcher who practiced hypnosis in Boston. The Bumpkins were told that, if anyone could help them remember a marketable UFO encounter, it would be Dr. Kopfkrummer, so they drove down to Boston to see him.

Dr. Kopfkrummer sat Barney, Betty, and Poopsey down on three separate couches and began the hypnosis session. He asked them to count backwards from 100 to zero—except for Poopsey, who could only count from seven to zero by tapping her paw. Almost as soon as the counting began, all three were in a deep hypnotic trance.

In order to make sure they were in a deep trance, or perhaps just to entertain himself, Dr. Kopfkrummer made the Bumpkins do all the silly things that hypnotized people are asked to do in night club shows. For example, he had Barney, a very conservative man, get up on the coffee table and dance the "funky chicken." He then brought Betty out into the hallway to sing "What Do You Do with a Drunken Sailor?" at the top of her lungs. Finally, Dr. Kopfkrummer convinced Poopsey that she was a cat and made Barney bark like a dog and chase her out on to the window ledge.

All of these incidents were carefully videotaped just in case the Bumpkins were reluctant to share the royalties from their story with the good doctor. After these preparations, Kopfkrummer began questioning his patients, as follows:

Dr. Kopfkrummer: Okay, Barney, you can stop barking now. Barney, I want you to tell me about the night you and Betty saw the flying saucer. You will remember everything that happened that night as if it were happening right now. You have complete and total recall of even the smallest details. Nothing will escape your memory. Do you understand me, Barney?

Barney: Yes. I remember everything.

Dr. K.: Good. Now tell me what you were wearing that night.

Barney: I don't remember.

Dr. K.: Never mind. Tell me what happened when you first noticed the flying saucer.

Barney: I was driving. It was very dark and there were lots of stars out. I remember Betty told me one of the stars was following us.

Dr. K.: Do you remember that Betty?

Betty: (In a mock Irish accent) *"What do you do with a drunken sailor, what do you do with a drunken sailor, what do you do with a drunken sailor, early in the mornin'."*

Dr. K.: Betty, I want you to stop singing now and concentrate on the night, three years ago, when you and Barney saw a flying saucer.

Betty: (in her normal voice) Yes, I remember.

Abduction by the Aliens: The Bumpkin Story

Dr. K.: Tell me what you saw.

Betty: It was late and we were driving home in the dark. I was looking up at the sky when I noticed that one of the stars, a very bright one, was following us. Poopsey and I were very worried.

Dr. K.: You were worried about the star following you?

Betty: No, we were just curious about that. We were worried about Lucy.

Dr. K.: Lucy?

Betty: Yes. The "I Love Lucy" show. It was our favorite show. We had never missed an episode, but it was getting late and it looked like we weren't going to be home in time to see it. We were very disappointed. Isn't that right, Poopsey?

Poopsey: (whines affirmatively).

(Note how Dr. Kopfkrummer is careful not to make any suggestions that could lead the Bumpkins into imagining things about the encounter. That is why his questions are so nonspecific.)

Dr. K.: When did the aliens land and take you aboard their flying saucer for a medical examination?

Betty: Oh, that happened around 12:30 in the morning.

Barney: What time was that?

Dr. K.: She said 12:30 in the morning. Do you agree with that, Barney?

Barney: Okay. Sounds good to me.

Dr. K.: Now, Betty, I want you to tell me exactly what the spaceship looked like when you saw it land.

Betty: Spaceship? Oh, *that* spaceship. Well, it was large and round and very bright, like it was glowing or something. It was shaped sort of like a . . . like a saucer with windows, you know, like you read about in those books.

Dr. K.: What books? You haven't been reading flying saucer books have you, Betty?

Betty: Oh, no, doctor. I've never read a book on flying saucers. I've never even heard of flying saucers.

Dr. K.: That's better. Now can you describe to me what the aliens looked like.

Betty: They had large eyes, like an insect. They looked a lot like grasshoppers.

Dr. K.: Are you sure they didn't look more like crickets?

Betty: Yes, they could have been crickets, too? I guess you're right. We'll call them cricket men.

Dr. K.: Excellent. And what were these cricket men wearing, Betty?

Betty: Well, they had black uniforms, and they had large jumping legs, just like real crickets.

Dr. K.: No, Betty, that's too far out. They had bodies more like humans, only shorter. And they were wearing blue-colored jumpsuits, like a doctor wears in surgery.

Betty: Yes, okay, crickets in blue jumpsuits. Like doctors wear.

Dr. K.: Good. And what did they do after they took you and Barney into their spaceship?

Betty: They gave us a medical examination. And that really bothered me.

Dr. K.: Why did the examination bother you?

Betty: Well, I had already had an exam a few weeks before and I wasn't sure if my insurance would cover this extra one? I'm only covered for one exam every six months unless I become

Abduction by the Aliens: The Bumpkin Story 77

ill, so I asked them if I could have a note for my insurance that said I was ill.

Dr. K.: And what did they say?

Betty: They didn't understand. They told me they don't have insurance on their planet.

Dr. K.: Barney, how did you feel while this was going on?

Barney: I was worried about how Poopsey was going to take it. You see, she's really scared of crickets, 'cause they can jump higher than she can.

Dr. K.: Don't worry about Poopsey. She stayed in the car the whole time.

Barney: In the car. That's right, now I remember. Poopsey was in the car.

Poopsey: (whines in agreement).

Dr. K.: How did you feel about the exam they gave you and Betty?

Barney: Well, I was really nervous because we were on vacation and I didn't expect anybody to give me an exam, you see. And, since I didn't know about it, I didn't have any time to study for it.

I knew I wasn't doing too well when they asked me what the capital of Nebraska was. I didn't think that was a fair question because I had never been to Nebraska....

Dr. K.: Barney, it was a *medical* exam. The aliens were giving you a *medical* exam. Aren't you paying attention?

Barney: Oh. A medical exam. Why would they do that? I wasn't even sick, was I?

Dr. K.: Never mind, Barney. Let's just say you slept through the whole thing.

Barney: That's right, I slept through the whole thing.

78 Flying Saucers Are Everywhere

Slowly but surely, Dr. Kopfkrummer's hypnosis enabled Betty and Barney to recall the missing hours. The result was an incredibly detailed account of an encounter between simple earth people and space travelers from another star system. The Bumpkins went on to explain how the aliens spoke to them without moving their lips, as though they were telepaths, or perhaps very clever ventriloquists. The aliens even showed Betty a star map and pointed out their home base, a star called Beta Gesticulate in the constellation of Herpes. Betty drew a replica of the map under hypnosis. A copy of it is shown in figure 6A.

Later in the hypnosis session, Betty told Dr. Kopfkrummer about her conversation with the leader of the aliens, who revealed some interesting things about their purpose for being on Earth.

Dr. Kopfkrummer: Betty, did the aliens tell you why they had come to Earth?

Betty: Yes. After the medical exam, the leader told me they were here to open up new trade routes. He said they wanted to start trading with Earth. That's what the medical exam was for, to see what kind of creatures we were so they could figure out how gullible we would be.

Dr. K.: Did he tell you what they had to sell?

Betty: Eventually, yes. But first he asked me some questions. He said, "Do you work at a boring job five days a week?" and I said yes. Then he said, "Do you feel like you don't have control of your time?" and I said yes. Then he said, "If I were to show you a product that could achieve love, happiness, and world peace while making you the richest woman on your planet, would you be interested in becoming a distributor for this product?"

Dr. K.: What was the product they wanted to distribute?

Betty: Well, he said he had this book that contained all I needed to know about love, happiness, world peace, and all the secrets of the universe. He showed it to me but it was written in some

Figure 6A
Betty Bumpkin's Star Map

strange language that I didn't recognize. He told me that for just a $10,000 investment, I could have the English translation and they would make me a distributor for the entire planet. Of course, I told him Barney and I were only simple people and we didn't have that kind of money, so he told me he would accept a check because he trusted me.

I responded that I didn't even have that kind of money in the bank. If I did I might have given it to him because he was very convincing and, well, who wouldn't want a book like that from these space people? Then he said he would accept a credit card and I could pay it off in monthly installments, but I told him it was only the early sixties and credit cards were not yet in widespread use.

Dr. K.: How did he respond to that?

Betty: Well, he said that if I was not satisfied with the product, for any reason, I could have a complete refund after trying it for one full year. I told him again that there was no way I could afford to buy it even if I wanted to. By now I was starting to get suspicious, though. Even a simple country girl like me knows that he's going to be in another galaxy a year from now and there's no way I'd ever get my money back. So I told him to forget it.

Dr. K.: Did he persist?

Betty: Yes, he did. He took me over to this chart and showed me a little pyramid sketched on a drawing board. He drew little figures on the board next to the pyramid and described to me how I would get a percentage of the profits for everyone on Earth who I recruited to distribute their book. He drew figures with lots of zeros and said I would easily be the richest woman on Earth. He then added that, after the earth started colonizing other planets, I would get a percentage from all the colonies as well.

I told him that sounded very interesting but I didn't have the money, so there was no way I could pay him $10,000. He finally realized that I wasn't going to buy and he said that earth people were a hard sell.

Dr. K.: Did he say he tried to recruit other earth people?

Betty: Yes. He tried to recruit the Pharaohs to distribute his book thousands of years ago in Egypt, but they didn't seem to understand. They ended up building huge brick replicas of his pyramid chart, which were very impressive but missed his point entirely.

Dr. K.: Did the aliens have anything else to sell besides this book?

Betty: Yes. After he realized I didn't have a lot of money, he said he would sell me some little crystal trinkets for $10 apiece. I was about to buy one, just so I could show people that I had really been there, but then something strange happened. I was looking through my purse and some paper clips fell out. I keep a little box of them in my purse for use at work. Well, the aliens saw these paper clips and they acted like it was the most wonderful thing they had ever seen. They asked me if I would trade the box of paper clips for some of the crystals, so I said I would. Apparently paper clips are very valuable on their planet.

The aliens returned the Bumpkins to their car and telepathically told them they would forget everything about the encounter. The only evidence of the aliens was the crystal trinkets that Betty had bartered from them, but she just assumed she had bought them at a gift shop.

After the hypnosis sessions were over, the Bumpkin story was published in a bestselling book, followed by a *very* bad TV movie. The Bumpkin case was so widely documented that it became a standard by which all subsequent UFO abductions were based, and before long, cricket-faced aliens were popping up all over the world.

Seven

Invasion of the Cricket Men and Other Alien Species

As soon as the Bumpkins' book hit the bestseller lists, the world found itself in the midst of another major UFO flap. Bookstores set up special shelves for all the UFO titles. And filling those shelves were dozens of books about abductions, all of them based on the Betty and Barney Bumpkin case, but each one adding its own unique touch to the phenomenon. In fact, the variety of abduction stories led one serious UFOlogist to remark, "As soon as I think I have these aliens figured out, they add a whole new twist to the mystery. Its almost as if someone's making all this up as they go along."

But the aliens were too busy to be figured out, as police Sergeant Herman Schizmann soon discovered. Sergeant Schizmann, an officer from Chaffland, Nebraska, had never heard of the Bumpkins' book before his UFO encounter in 1967, even though it was on the top of the bestseller lists for most of that year. In fact, Herman Schizmann had never even heard of flying saucers before 1967, due to the fact that he had been living in a cave most of his life. But on the night of June 27, Sergeant

Schizmann had an experience that made him one of the most famous abductees in UFO history.

After finishing his shift patrolling the Chaffland doughnut shops, Schizmann wrote in his police log that he had encountered a strange, saucer-like object hovering above his cruiser in a remote area of town. The sergeant also noted that he couldn't account for thirty minutes of time although he only remembered dozing off for about five minutes. Sergeant Schizmann then went home and tried to forget about the incident, but he developed a chronic bed-wetting problem that eventually led him to seek professional help.

After mentioning his problem to a journalist who was interested in his UFO story, Schizmann was recommended to Dr. Leonard Swindling, the staff hypnotist for a syndicated television game show. Dr. Swindling agreed to hypnotize the sergeant to help him uncover the missing time. Under hypnosis, Schizmann discovered that, during the lost half hour, he had experienced an incredible, three-hour encounter with aliens from a nearby galaxy. The encounter could well have gone longer except that Dr. Swindling had another appointment to keep.

Sergeant Schizmann's aliens looked remarkably like the ones in the Bumpkin case except that they wore lamp shades on their heads (see figure 7A). But they had the same probing eyes, which Sergeant Schizmann compared to the eyes of a praying mantis. Schizmann even described the "blue pajamas" worn by the aliens, similar to the "medical suits" described by Betty Bumpkin. But, instead of giving Schizmann a medical exam, these aliens told him they were having an interplanetary pajama party and invited him to take a ride with them around the solar system.

Schizmann said his aliens, who "talked through their minds," appeared to be teenagers who had snuck out with their parents' spaceship for a joy ride. He said they stopped in a field to smoke some grape vines, then flew out to the edge of the solar system to toilet paper the planet Neptune. When it started to get late, the young aliens pressed their ship to fly faster than the speed of light so time would go backward. This

Invasion of the Cricket Men and Other Alien Species

Figure 7A
The Schizmann Aliens

would account for Schizmann's three-hour experience while only a half hour had passed on Earth.[1]

Schizmann went on to become the toast of the talk show circuit for several months, until his integrity came into question after he claimed he could predict the future by reading bird droppings. Schizmann's career really took a turn for the worse when he predicted that Greenland would go to war with Russia over ice-fishing rights. After being driven out of his hometown by a mob of nonbelievers, Schizmann settled in a forest in Oregon where he was last seen living in a tree house and trying to communicate with woodpeckers using a modified Morse code.

---

1. Einstein's theory of relativity states that, if a bus were traveling faster than the speed of light, time would go backward for the passengers inside. However, due to the effects of "brain dilation," the driver of the bus would continue to blatantly ignore traffic laws.

Figure 7B
Wynona Tanner's Aliens

* * *

On the night of July 23, 1968, about a year after Schizmann's story first made the news, Mrs. Wynona Tanner of Yarnsville, Kentucky, saw a flash of light in her backyard. Tanner, a single mother, had just put her children to bed and was watching television at the time. "At first I thought it was lightning," she later said, "and I wasn't worried about it, but I had this strange, subconscious urge to undergo a medical exam."

Wynona went to open her front door and was met there by a group of shortish aliens covered in foil-like space suits (see Figure 7B). She said her aliens had small boxes that looked like transistor radios attached to their left ear, nearly two decades before the invention of the Sony Walkman. Wynona invited the aliens to come in and shoot her with their paralyzer beam, which they did before examining her and all the electrical appliances in her home.

Invasion of the Cricket Men and Other Alien Species   87

The Tanner aliens took a special interest in Wynona's telephone and, using the standard telepathic communications, they asked her to explain what it was. Wynona was floated over to the phone and released from her temporary paralysis in order to demonstrate how to make a call. She said the aliens were fascinated by the sounds of the dial tone and rotary clicks and, when she dialed a number that was busy, they began to dance to the beat of the busy signal. Before long the aliens were able to mimic the sound; they all went buzzing around her living room making busy signal noises.

When the festivities were over, the aliens told Wynona she would forget everything that had occurred, but they would be in touch with her by telephone. Wynona woke up the next morning and found herself lying on the living room floor with no memory at all of the aliens. However, when she called a friend and got a busy signal, her memory of the night before came back to her and she began dancing to the tone in front of her children.

Since dancing in front of children was illegal in her county, Wynona was arrested and declared legally insane. She currently resides in a mental hospital where she spends her time playing children's songs on a touch-tone, cellular telephone.

A somewhat different form of alien was described by Mrs. Virginia Tibbet, from Blue Moon, California. In late August of 1971, Mrs. Tibbet was awakened by a loud bang that seemed to come from just outside her house. Virginia looked out her bedroom window and saw a small, disc-shaped craft sitting on the lawn. She watched the craft as a door slid open and three humanoids emerged and floated toward her. Virginia said these aliens wore helmets that looked "just like goldfish bowls" (see Figure 7C). The aliens then put a spell on Virginia, commanding her to open her window and let them in.

The next day, Virginia described the startling events that took place in her living room as her husband continued to sleep. "They told me they had been searching the entire universe for a way to get their heads out of those goldfish bowls," Virginia

Figure 7C
The "Fish-Bowl" Aliens

recalled. She said she offered to let them use her hammer to break out of the helmets.

"One of the aliens took the hammer and carefully broke open his helmet," she said. "He looked very relieved that he was finally out of it and I asked him how they had all gotten their heads stuck in the first place." Instead of answering her, however, the alien asked Virginia if she had any goldfish.

"I said yes, and pointed to my fish bowl across the room," she said. "Well, then he walked over, stuck his head right into my fish bowl and ate all three of my goldfish. I said, 'What did you do that for?' but he just belched and then broke my fish bowl with the hammer." The alien then freed his companions from their bowls and the three of them left as mysteriously as they had arrived, this time without helmets.

It is significant that these aliens, unlike most, did not cause Virginia to forget her encounter. It should also be noted that the belch she heard was an actual sound and not a telepathic communication.

In the early 1980s the number of abductions increased as the aliens became more daring in their methods. No longer were abductions limited to remote, wooded areas like northern New Hampshire or the Appalachian mountains. In 1983 an entire family was abducted from their suburban home in Chelsea Woods, Indiana, by a spacecraft that pulled right into their driveway. The fact that none of their neighbors saw the spaceship suggests that the aliens are capable of controlling the minds of potential witnesses with a form of selective blindness. Either that or the family just overreacted to a late-night horror movie they were watching. Anyway, the appearance and behavior of the aliens was noticeably different from the encounters reported in the early 1960s.

In 1982 a woman whom we'll call Petunia, because it's a humorous name, claimed she had been abducted while waiting for a trolley car in broad daylight. Petunia said these aliens had beaks and owl-like ears; they told her they drained power from the wires above the trolley cars. They also said they did not really look like owls but disguised themselves as such to avoid detection by the utility company which was trying to prosecute them for unpaid bills.

Later that same year a woman from Tulsa, Oklahoma, claimed her home had been invaded by five robot-like creatures who parked their spacecraft in her front yard and broke into her home despite a sophisticated alarm system. The woman, Mrs. Sarah Bovine, said one robot assaulted her microwave oven, another mutilated her coffee maker, and the other three appeared to be fighting over her portable vacuum cleaner. Mrs. Bovine has sued her insurance company to get them to cover her losses, claiming that alien invasions should be included under theft and vandalism. Her historic case is still in the courts but her book, *They Gang-Banged My Mini-Vac,* should be in bookstores any day now.

* * *

Abduction patterns in the latter half of the 1980s showed even more audacity on the part of the aliens, with some victims being abducted from heavily populated urban areas. One middle-aged woman recalled under hypnosis that she saw an alien spaceship hovering just outside the window of her apartment on the twenty-second floor of a New York City skyscraper. She said four cricket-men emerged from the ship and walked *right through the wall* into her living room where they implanted a tracking device into her earlobe. She said they used the device to locate her for a second abduction a few weeks later, at which time they actually floated *her* through the wall of the building and into their ship. The woman said she didn't feel anything unusual when passing through the wall with the aliens but she did experience severe headaches later when she tried to perform the same feat for some friends at a party.

Scores of other abduction cases have been documented where the aliens, and sometimes humans, walk right through the walls of their homes and into a spaceship. Before long, people were reporting that they were beamed right up to the saucers by an energy transporter like the one they use on "Star Trek." This was first documented with the case of Tom-Bob Gooberman, a lumberjack from Wandering Flakes, Utah.

Gooberman and five other lumberjacks were heading home at dusk on November 5, 1986, when they were startled by a brightly lit flying saucer that appeared above their jeep at treetop level. The jeep's engine stalled and the men all panicked except for Gooberman, who jumped out and walked toward the object. The witnesses said Gooberman raised his hand toward the object in the "live long and prosper" gesture made popular by Mr. Spock. When he did, a beam of light from the saucer shot down at him and he vanished into midair. The spaceship then flew away and the jeep engine started back up.

The lumberjacks were so frightened that they sped off and didn't stop until they got to the Wandering Flakes police station. Sheriff Gullivan said the men were all consistent in their use

Invasion of the Cricket Men and Other Alien Species 91

of the term "flying saucer," so he was convinced they were not making it up. The sheriff said, "When I heard their story I immediately bit off a chaw of tobacco and commenced to thinkin'." He set up a search-posse, which searched the area for two days but no trace of a posse could be found. After a short rest, they then started looking for Gooberman.

Finally, on the fourth day, Gooberman was found, stinking drunk, in a telephone booth, where he said he was hiding from Klingon warriors. Gooberman said he had been beamed aboard the Starship *Enterprise* when he vanished from the woods. The legendary vessel had fallen into a time warp while filming *Star Trek 17, The Very, Very Last and Final Frontier*. Gooberman said Captain Kirk and the crew of the *Enterprise* needed some help finding their way back to the future, and asked him to man the photon torpedoes while Mr. Spock computed the correct space-time coordinates. After they were finished, engineer Scotty thought he had done such a fine job that he treated Gooberman to some 200-year-old Scotch whiskey, which actually wouldn't have been made yet since it had come from the twenty-third century.

After he was beamed back to Earth, Gooberman said, the Klingons came after him to try to get some secrets about the *Enterprise*'s defense shields. He had hidden in the phone booth for two days while the Klingons searched the county for him. Gooberman was brought immediately to the sheriff's office and given a lie detector test. The polygraph expert who administered the test said his results indicated that "that must have been some very fine whiskey indeed."

Gooberman and his fellow witnesses were awarded $20,000 by *Flying Saucer Magazine* for the most convincing evidence yet that Klingons can't see through phone booths. In addition, their story was bought by The Cable Movie Network and made into one of the *worst* cable movies ever produced.

According to UFO researchers who tend to believe everything they read, over 5,000 people have been abducted by at least fifty different types of aliens. Some of the most common alien types are shown in figure 7D, but this is only a sampling.

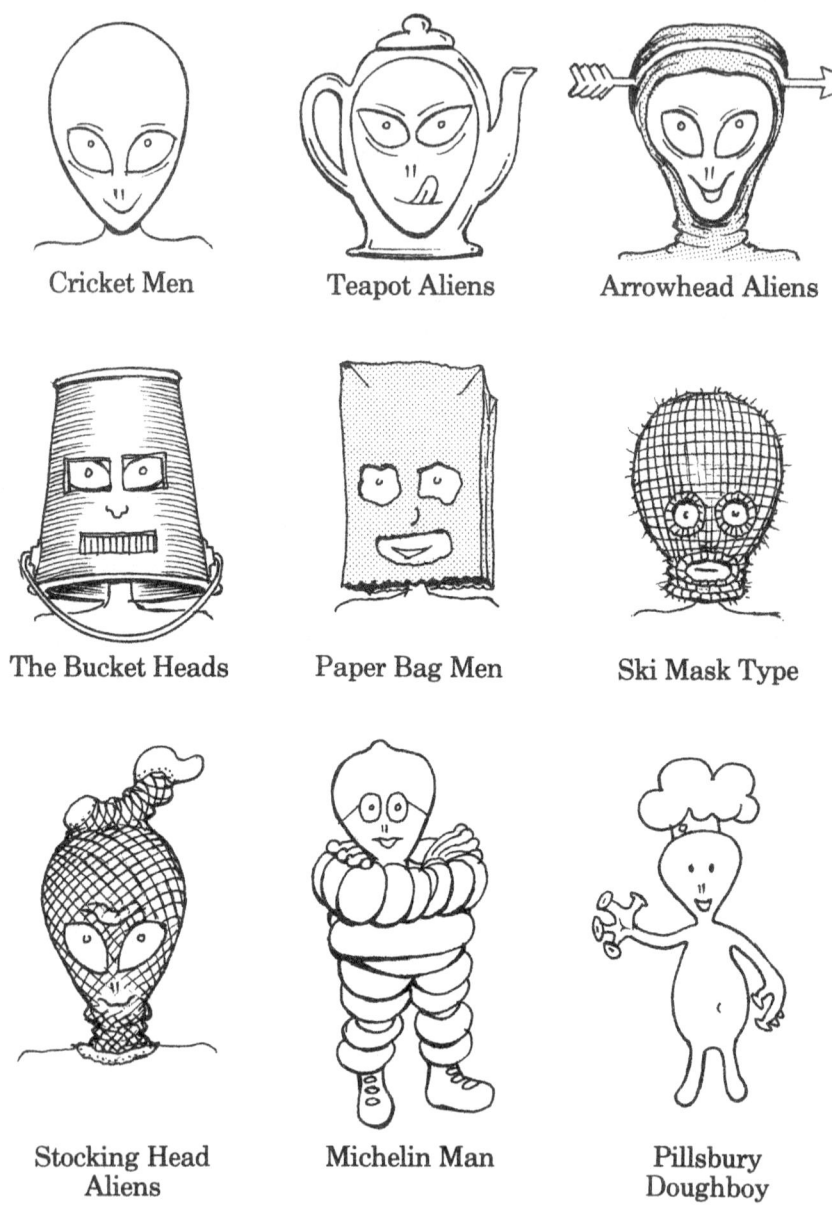

Figure 7D
Some Common Alien Types

Invasion of the Cricket Men and Other Alien Species 93

In addition, UFO experts estimate that, for every reported abduction, there are at least five more that have gone unreported, either because the abductees were forced to forget or because that number is a wildly inaccurate guess. But, just in case there are any latent abductees among the readers of this book, a quiz has been included that may be used to identify a possible abduction in your own past. Answers and scores are shown at the end of the chapter.

ARE YOU A UFO CONTACTEE?—A QUIZ

Yes/No Section

1. Do you have a goofy name like Herman, Barney, Petunia, or Tom-Bob?

2. Do you live or work in an area that could be called "the boondocks?"

3. Do you have recurring dreams about humanoid creatures with large eyes and leathery skin?

4. How do you know their skin is leathery if they have those jumpsuits on?

5. Have you ever seen, or thought you may have seen, the tooth fairy?

6. Do you get frequent nosebleeds? Do you whine about them a lot or do you take it like a man?

7. Do you ever wake up with unexplained welts or scabs on your body? Do you like to pick at them or do you cover them with a bandaid?

8. Do you believe in extrasensory perception? If so, what am I thinking right now?

9. Did you get picked on by the other kids in high school? Do you think I care?

10. Do you ever think the lyrics of a popular song have a special meaning that only you can interpret? If so, do you own any guns?

Multiple Choice

1. When you see news reports of Unidentified Flying Objects, how do you react?
    A. Assume it's a hoax
    B. Take the witness' word for it
    C. Go into a trance and start talking in a deep voice
    D. Turn the channel and watch "Wheel of Fortune"

2. When you read books about UFO abductions, how do you react?
    A. Assume its a hoax
    B. Believe it unless it is proven false
    C. Draw mustaches and genitalia on the aliens in the illustrations
    D. Look for the parts where the aliens get sexual with the earthlings

3. What is the level of your telepathic ability?
    A. I can occasionally tell what other people are thinking
    B. Other people can sometimes tell what I'm thinking
    C. I can rarely tell what I'm thinking

4. What is your favorite science fiction movie?
    A. *E.T.*
    B. *Close Encounters of the Third Kind*
    C. *Mars Needs Women*
    D. *The Naughty Cheerleaders from Venus*

5. What is the capital of Venus?
    A. Adonis
    B. Venus City
    C. Venezuela
    D. I cannot reveal that information at this time

Essay Question

1. What exactly are "the boondocks" anyway?

Invasion of the Cricket Men and Other Alien Species 97

Quiz Answers and Scores

Yes/No Section

1. Yes—5 points, No—0 points
2. Yes—5, No—0
3. Yes—5, No—0
4. Any answer—10 points
5. Yes—5, No—0
6. Yes—5, No—0;
   Whine about it—1, Take it like a man—5
7. Yes—10, No—0;
   Pick at them—5, Band-aid—10
8. Yes—5, No—0;
   If you said I was thinking of the number 7—15 extra points
9. Yes—0, No—0;
   If you said I don't care—5 extra points
10. Yes—10, No—0;
    If you own a gun, subtract 20 points

Multiple Choice Section

1. A—0 points, B—2 points, C—5 points, D—10 points
2. A—0, B—5, C—10, D—15
3. A—5, B—5, C—10
4. A—5, B—10, C—15, D—25
5. A—2, B—0, C—3, D—15

Essay Question

1. If you said that a "boondock" is a place to dock your "boon," then subtract 20 points. For any other answer, add 10 points.

Interpreting Your Score

0 to 50 points:	Not a likely contactee.
51 to 100 points:	There's potential. Join a UFO club.
101 or higher:	You are very likely to be contacted by the aliens and would easily qualify for jury duty.

Eight

The Big Government Cover-Up and Radar-Resistant Cheese

If aliens have been flying around and landing on the earth for so long, we may be inclined to ask why they haven't contacted the government. After all, in science fiction books, the first thing an alien life form does when it visits Earth is to ask to see the people in charge, usually the local television station. In this chapter we will examine how our government has been trying to cover up all evidence of the alien visits and how paranoid we should be about it.

In order to come to an objective, rational, and unbiased conclusion about the U.S. government, people must first realize that the government is out to get them. Anyone who has ever been audited by the IRS or unfairly convicted of a traffic violation understands this, but many citizens who have been able to avoid such problems may be foolish enough to trust their government. This would be a big mistake. For one thing, you would have no one to blame your problems on; but more important, you might believe the government when they tell you there is no such thing as UFOs, and such beliefs could seriously impair the career of UFOlogists.

Fortunately, most Americans know better than to trust their government, but few realize just how far Uncle Sam has gone in covering up the truth about flying saucers. The first government involvement with UFOs began with our founding fathers when they were drafting the Constitution in Philadelphia. Many of the delegates to the Constitutional Convention had been visited by the aliens and had even sought their advice on how to start a new country. But the delegates feared that if the people in their home states knew of this they might not give them credit for drafting the Constitution, and they wouldn't get to have cities and turnpikes named after them. For this reason, all the delegates to the Constitutional Convention were required to sign the affidavit shown below, written in the Olde English script:

> We, the Delegatef to the Conftitutional Convention, do folemnly fwear that we will difpute, deny and belittle any Referenfe to the role that Alienf or Unidentified Flying Objectf have played in the drafting of our Conftitution. We alfo promife to fpeak wif a tewwible lifp in accordanfe wif the Cuftom of our Time.

This affidavit was the firft, I mean the first, document in our nation's history to be classified top secret. It was hidden in the attic of the National Archives after the Constitution was ratified and not discovered until the 1970s, when it was found by a lawyer for the Nixon administration which was trying to dig up some dirt on the Democrats.

The tradition of a government UFO cover-up was further promoted by our first president. During George Washington's second term in office, the newspapers reported a miniature UFO flap that occurred in the nation's capital. After several reliable citizens at the time had admitted to seeing flying saucers, the president was asked his opinion on the matter. Setting off a history of presidential denial, Washington explained the UFOs away with the excuse that people were probably just seeing the cherry pies that he enjoyed throwing across the Potomac River now and then.

We also know that President Andrew Jackson ("Old Hickory Head") was assisted by aliens in his heroic defeat of British soldiers during the War of 1812. Hundreds of witnesses on both sides of the war reported seeing flying saucers swoop down from the skies and come to the aid of Jackson's heavily outnumbered troops. Yet, when questioned about the alien assistance, Jackson claimed that the lights people had seen in the skies were a new kind of cannon ball which he threatened to use against anyone who questioned him any further about it.

It has been suggested that President John F. Kennedy ("Old Hot 'n' Horny") and his brothers often had covert encounters with alien women. An aide to the Kennedys claims that, shortly after the Cuban missile crisis, he walked into the Blue Room of the White House to find the president and Attorney General Robert Kennedy floating around the room in midair with two green-skinned women with antennae. The aide said he suspected that the president's wife knew about the affair, because Mrs. Kennedy made her husband swear he would not send a rocket to Mars during his term.

The aliens are also said to have been an instrumental part of President Richard Nixon's "secret solution" for peace in Vietnam. According to sources close to "Old Tricky Dick," the plan was to have a squadron of saucers fly over North Vietnamese air space and spell out the words: "We Surrender." Unfortunately the words were mistranslated and the saucer squadron actually spelled out: "Paul McCartney is Dead," which set off rumors throughout the world but did nothing to end the war.

This controversy goes well beyond the White House, however. The CIA is heavily involved in a cover-up of the flying saucer phenomenon. I know this because, when I called CIA headquarters and asked them about it, they immediately denied everything. For further proof, I have obtained TOP SECRET DOCUMENTS concerning the cover-up of a crashed saucer that was recovered in the New Mexico desert in 1984.

According to my sources, the crash was witnessed by a cactus farmer who watched the vehicle plunge from the sky while he was tending his crops. The farmer immediately called

102   Flying Saucers Are Everywhere

the Air Force on a cellular phone which he happened to have in his tractor. The Air Force responded by evacuating the area and holding a formal dinner party, where high-ranking officers drank grain alcohol from a "grog" bowl until they passed out. The next morning, they confiscated all evidence, including the bodies of four dead aliens and several comatose officers. The corpses were taken to a super-secret laboratory at Wright-Patterson Air Force Base, where they were studied and occasionally leased out for use in science fiction movies.

The following document, which was stolen from the trash

cans of the *National Enquirer*, proves beyond doubt that the crash was covered up by the highest levels of government intelligence officers:

TOP SECRET/CRICKET

THIS FILE IS CLASSIFIED TOP SECRET FOR USE ONLY BY AUTHORIZED PROJECT CRICKET PERSONNEL. ANYONE WHO USES THIS FILE FOR UNAUTHORIZED PURPOSES MAY BE PUNISHED BY HAVING HIS KNUCKLES SLAPPED WITH A RULER BY HUSKY CATHOLIC NUNS WHO WILL THEN PULL HIM BY THE EARS INTO THE BACK ROOM, GRAB HIM BY THE HAIR AROUND THE TEMPLES, WHERE IT IS MOST SENSITIVE, AND SHAKE HIS HEAD BACK AND FORTH WHILE THEY SCOLD HIM AND LECTURE HIM ABOUT THE SEVERITY OF HIS OFFENSE. THE OFFENDER WILL THEN BE FORCED TO BEND OVER AND GRAB HIS ANKLES AND . . . , WELL, TRUST US, YOU DO **NOT** WANT TO USE THESE DOCUMENTS FOR ANY UNAUTHORIZED PURPOSES.

This warning is in accordance with U.S. Code 216A, Title 14, Section 913, Room 26B (second drawer from the top in the desk by the door). It is enforced by Executive Order 10826, The Mother Superior Oversight Directive.

Subject: Recommendations of Project Cricket
From: Lt. Colonel Oliver North
To: CIA Director William Casey
Date: 23 March 1985

As you know, on the afternoon of 15 November 1984 a crashed flying saucer was retrieved from a private cactus farm in the New Mexico desert. The saucer wreckage and the bodies of four alien occupants were taken to Wright-Patterson Air Force Base for analysis and economic exploitation. Project Cricket was set up, with me as its chairman, to determine if this situation provided us a chance to engage in any illegal, covert activities.

The scientists from Project Cricket have analyzed the bodies of the alien crash victims and have found their flesh to be similar in texture to pork bellies, but containing slightly more gristle. Our scientists have been able to clone the alien flesh and several major food companies have expressed an interest in licensing the material.

In addition, the pieces of wreckage from the hull of the flying saucer have been carefully scrutinized. Our scientists believe it is made of hardened Gouda cheese. After extensive tests with this substance, we have concluded that it would provide a cheap and effective material for the construction of radar-resistant aircraft. Marketing analysts have suggested that this, too, could be licensed to private businesses for substantial sums of money.

The Cricket Committee recommends the following actions:

- licensing the commercial rights to the cloned alien flesh and the aircraft material to private businesses

- using the proceeds to cover the costs of arming Third World terrorists so they'll think we're their friends

- using the original alien bodies for leverage in negotiations with the alien leaders for the return of the various aircraft and ships which they have been taking from the Bermuda Triangle over the past few decades.

It has also been suggested that we allow the aliens to abduct our President so they can erase his memory and provide him with "plausible deniability." Unless we hear from you in the next three days, we will proceed with the above recommendations.

My sources have confirmed that the license to market the cloned alien flesh was sold to the McDonald's Corporation and used in the chain's highly successful McRib Sandwich promotion. In addition, the cheese-based substance from which the saucer was made was licensed to the Northrop Corporation, which is using it to build the radar-evading stealth bomber. There are also reports that Colonel North traded some of the spacecraft material to Iran in exchange for some flying carpets, but that could not be confirmed. As for the negotiations with the aliens over the Bermuda Triangle: at the time of this writing they have been stalled by a disagreement over the actual shape and boundaries of the dreaded region (see chapter 9).

As impressive as TOP SECRET DOCUMENTS may be, nothing could be more convincing than the testimony of U.S. astronauts who say they have seen unidentified flying objects on their missions in outer space. Astronauts have been reporting UFOs since the early days of the Mercury program and their sightings have continued right up to recent space shuttle missions; yet our government has consistently denied that any extraterrestrial vehicles have been encountered. Some astronauts have even taken pictures of flying saucers, but as soon as the film is turned over to NASA it is mysteriously lost.

During America's first suborbital flight, astronaut Alan "Gus" Shepard reported that he saw a large, yellow object trailing his capsule. Whenever the mysterious object came into view, "Gus" would snap pictures of it on his in-flight camera and fax them back to ground controllers. Mission Control in Houston was very concerned about the safety of the nation's first astronaut, especially when Shepard told them he was hearing voices in his head that kept saying "Mars needs women."

The mystery was finally solved when analysis of the photographs revealed that the object was a column of frozen urine that had attached itself to the spacecraft when flushed through the capsule's zero-gravity suction toilet. The analysis also showed that Shepard had been drinking too much whiskey the night before his flight, which might account for the voices that he heard.

During the flight of *Gemini 5,* astronauts Leroy "Gus" Cooper and Charles "Gus" Conrad were supposed to rendezvous with a previously launched Right Guard aerosol rocket. The docking procedure worked perfectly, until "Gus" Conrad got out for a space walk and noticed that the object they had docked with was covered with ice. After analyzing the ice with a spectrograph, the astronauts realized they had not docked with the

Right Guard vehicle after all but with "Gus" Shepard's frozen urine.

The mission wasn't a complete loss, however. The object provided an opportunity for experiments that later became the basis for the Strategic Defense Initiative. The frozen urine was tracked in its orbit while scientists on Earth aimed laser beams at it and propelled it toward imaginary Russian missiles. These tests were an important prelude to the 1980s "Star Wars" projects involving "smart rocks," "brilliant pebbles," and "brighter-than-average piss crystals," the results of which are still highly classified.

The Apollo project, which landed several "Guses" on the moon, also had its share of UFO sightings. During the flight of *Apollo 14,* for example, Commander Thomas "Gus" Stafford reported seeing a UFO just after he and his partners docked the LEM, or Linguini Exchange Module, with the SCM, or Spam-in-a-Can Module. Stafford notified Mission Control that he spotted a "bogey" on the "starboard" side of the space capsule. In astronaut lingo, a "bogey" could be an unidentified aircraft, one stroke over par in a golf match or, in this case, a large, floating booger that was set loose in the cockpit by astronaut Walter "Gus" Cunningham when he sneezed. After extensive consultations with Deke "Gus" Slayton back at Mission Control, the astronauts were able to capture this "bogey" with some adhesive tape and a Kleenex.

Even the first woman in space, Sally "Gus" Ride, saw a UFO during her historic space shuttle mission. Ride and her fellow astronauts were on their twenty-fourth orbit when they noticed what they thought was a large, foul-smelling comet on a collision course with their shuttle. After taking evasive maneuvers with the shuttle's retrorockets, "Gus" Ride analyzed the object through a telescope. Her analysis revealed that "Gus" Shepard's urine had been encountered once again, and this time it showed evidence of a bladder infection. Shepard was notified of the problem at his home. He reported to a local clinic where he was treated with antibiotics and released.

These anecdotes reveal that every major U.S. space program has resulted in reports of unidentified flying objects, all of which were suspiciously suppressed by the government. Of course, none of these reports prove the existence of alien spaceships. In fact, all they really prove is that a tasteless writer will go out of his way to milk a frozen urine joke. But I still think the government knows more about flying saucers than they're letting on.

During the mid-1970s, Senator Barry Goldwater tried to get to the bottom of the UFO cover-up by holding Senate hearings on the issue. Due to a parliamentary procedure, the UFO hearings were combined with hearings on the funding of the National Endowment for the Arts. Nevertheless, Senator Goldwater had an all-star cast of witnesses and government officials ready for a thorough discussion on the government's involvement with UFOs. For a while, it looked as if Air Force officers and CIA agents were about to be forced, under oath, to tell the world all they knew about their extraterrestrial connections. Unfortunately, the combination of topics caused some problems.

When the hearings opened, Senator Orrin Hatch began reading a pornographic story about an alien abduction from a back issue of *Hustler* magazine. As he read aloud, Senator Jesse Helms distributed pictures of baked potato sculptures from an art museum in Idaho. Senator Helms insisted that the potato sculptures, when viewed from a certain angle, in just the right light, looked like alien genitalia.

This titillating testimony compelled anchorman Tom Brokaw to cut short his vacation so he could cover the hearings on live television because, as he said, "the public has a right to know." Then, on an NBC News Special, Brokaw interviewed a woman from the Society for the Prevention of Vegetable Abuse, who claimed that the way the senators were fondling baked potatoes at the hearings was an outrageous form of sexual assault, if not outright rape.

The controversy became the center of media attention for a short time. The senators took the opportunity to double NEA funding, and to set up, in each of their states, investigative commissions on the potential sizes and shapes of alien sex organs. After that, however, the committee disintegrated into chaos and the hearings were finally canceled due to low Nielsen ratings. Since Senator Goldwater's witnesses were never called to testify, the public missed out on their best chance ever to discover what their government had been hiding from them. At the time, however, no one cared, because the nation had temporarily lost interest in UFOs and was following another media obsession: sexually transmitted diseases in baked potatoes.

But why, we have to wonder, has our government kept UFO information secret for so long? Why can't they just admit that alien beings are visiting Earth? Are they afraid it would cause a wave of panic that would sweep across the country? Do they fear that we will learn the secrets of the alien's anti-gravity drive and put the big oil companies out of business? Or perhaps they're afraid we'll become one with the universe and eliminate the need for a burgeoning bureaucracy.

These are all marketable possibilities and books have already been written on all of them. But perhaps we could allow ourselves to speculate a little further. Perhaps, if we try real hard, we can come up with:

FIVE REASONS WHY YOU'RE BETTER OFF *NOT* KNOWING THE TRUTH ABOUT FLYING SAUCERS:

1. You might find out that your entire life is just a discarded segment that was edited out of an alien's dream.

2. The aliens might teach us to read minds and everyone would hear those hit songs that are always playing inside your head, only it would sound like *you* were singing them.

3. You would find out that your last sexual encounter was watched and recorded by aliens who made it into a holographic film that won the Martian equivalent of an Academy Award for Best Comedy.

The Big Government Cover-Up   109

4. You might find out that our civilization reached its cultural peak with "Doogie Howser, M.D.," and that it can only go downhill from there.

5. You might find out that the Ayatollah Khomeini was right, that Islam really is the one true religion.

If any one of the above reasons is true, then perhaps we should give the government more credit. Maybe we should thank the Air Force and the CIA for allowing us to live our lives in relative peace, for not ruining our fantasy that the UFOs are here to bring peace on Earth, and to raise us to a higher level of cosmic awareness. Maybe we should respect the authorities and, even if we don't always agree with them, at least appreciate that they are doing what they feel is best for us common citizens.

But, personally, I'd prefer to keep calling them dirt-eating slugs.

Nine

The Bermuda Triangle and Other Dangerous Polygons

Another important UFOlogy topic that ranks right up there with the abduction experience is the Bermuda Triangle. Everyone has heard the macabre stories of how ships and planes have mysteriously disappeared from this region, only to show up a few years later in bestselling books and tacky TV specials. Like most other UFOlogists, I have spent several hours pondering the possible reasons for these mysterious goings-on, partly because this unearthly enigma is related to the UFO phenomenon, but mostly because I wanted this book to have an even ten chapters.

The Bermuda Triangle is bounded by a line that extends from Bermuda south to Puerto Rico, then northwest to Miami, Florida, then northeast back to Bermuda, and then directly west to Casablanca, Morocco; from there, it heads way south to Tierra Del Fuego in South America, then back north to Abilene, Texas, and then it arcs into Oklahoma and across the midwest, until it ends up in a large dumpster behind the Burger King at a shopping mall in Paramus, New Jersey.

A picture of this notorious region is shown in figure 9A.

This is not technically a triangle, as those of you who have studied geometry may have realized by now; but, since it would be rather clumsy to refer to it as the Bermuda-Triangle-Surrounded-by-an-Open-Ended-Curve-Topped-Para-Trapezoid, it is usually just called The Bermuda Triangle.

While figure 9A is the most commonly accepted definition of the Triangle, it is not the only one. The exact borders of this infamous region have been the subject of controversy for centuries. The British, for example, have long referred to it as an oval-shaped zone, while the French say it is a square. The more precise Japanese insist it is a fractal, snowflake-shaped area and the Russians claim it can only be described as a large, sprawling amoeboid. In 1977, the United Nations set up the Committee on Border Specifications for Regions of Mysterious Disappearances to settle this dispute, but, so far, all they have done is debate who has the rights to commercial exploitation of the area. Figure 9B (1-4) shows some of the more humorous shapes and boundaries suggested for this dreaded territory. For the sake of simplicity, I will continue to call it the Bermuda Triangle.

The most famous disappearance ever recorded in the Bermuda Triangle occurred on December 5, 1945. On that day, five TBM Avenger bomber planes left Fort Lauderdale, Florida, on a routine exercise to determine how well the pilots could fly after drinking rum and cokes all night. The sea and the sky were perfectly calm that day, except for an approaching tropical storm named Dweezle, which no one knew about because only female storms were recognized in those days.

The pilots of the five TBMs, collectively known as the Bacardi Squadron, because that was their favorite beverage, performed their maneuvers perfectly for the first part of the flight. They followed their leader in a close wing-to-wing pattern, and then they all opened their hatches to see if they could spit at each other while still in formation. Everyone appeared to be having a great time. One of the junior officers was overheard reporting that he had hit the plane next to him with his spit, so it was his turn to decide their next endeavor.

The Bermuda Triangle and Other Dangerous Polygons

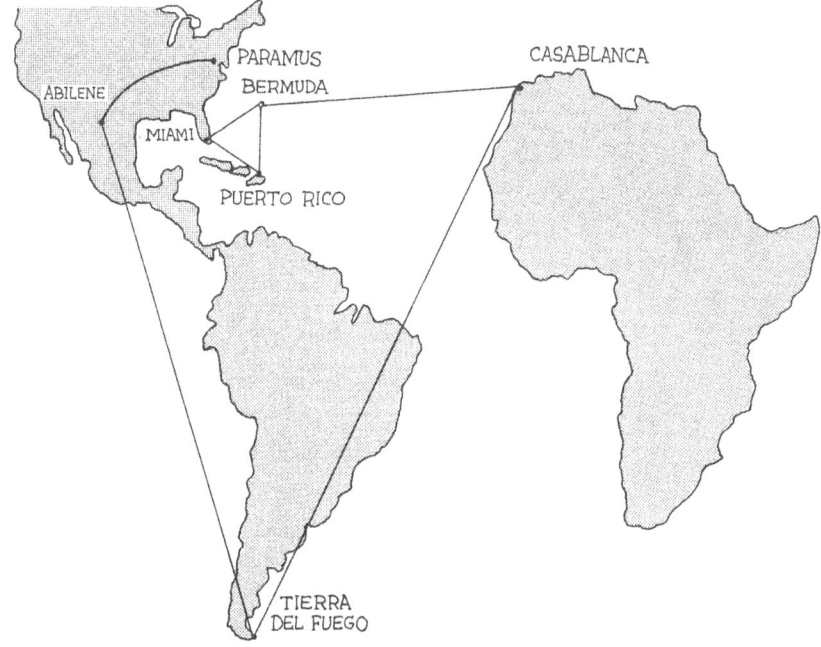

Figure 9A
The Bermuda Triangle

No one knows for sure what happened next to the Bacardi Squadron, which leaves it wide open to speculation that flying saucers were involved. An officer in the Fort Lauderdale control tower says he heard one of the pilots instruct his peers to go into a spiral nose dive. He then heard another pilot exclaim: "You didn't say 'Simon says.' " That was the last the control tower heard from the doomed Avengers.

When the squadron failed to report back to base at the scheduled time, the commander sent out a search-and-rescue team consisting of three dozen sonar-equipped fruit bats.

Eerily, the bats also disappeared.

This prompted the Navy to declare a state of emergency, and the local news media began speculating that the Bacardi Squadron might have flown through a hole in the sky. A mas-

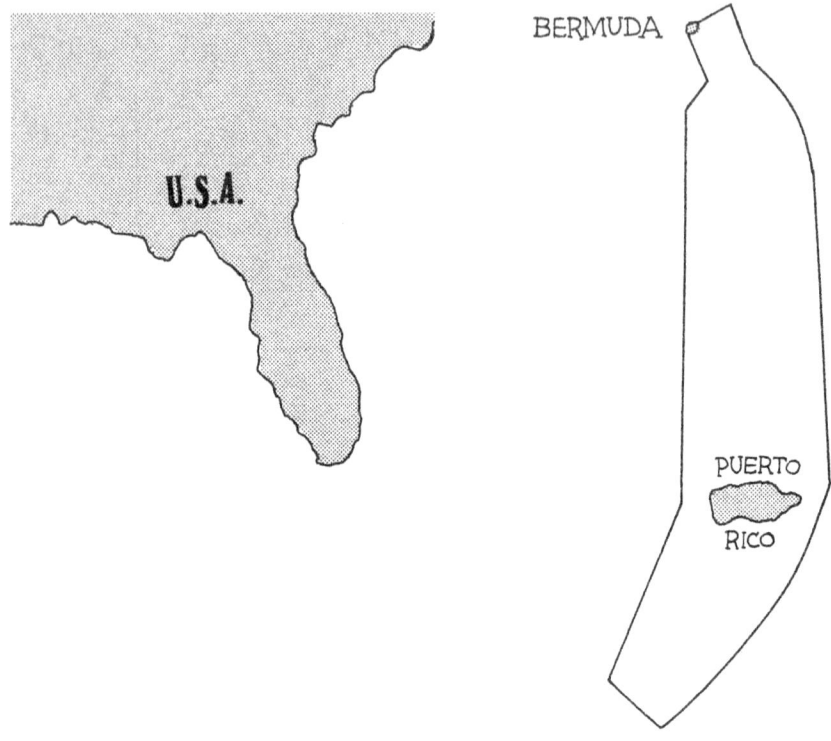

Figure 9B(1)
The Bermuda Banana

sive search mission was put together involving hundreds of ships, planes, and seafaring bloodhounds. Within a few days the team had searched 350,000 square miles, but not one shred of the missing squadron was found. On the bright side, however, no one else was lost, after the bats. There was a close call when one plane, due to an instrument error, actually did fly through a hole in the sky, but it was escorted safely back by Luke Skywalker and his faithful wookee, Chewbacca. Even Skywalker said he hadn't seen the missing Avengers, though, so that pretty much eliminated the hole-in-the-sky theory.

But what *did* happen to the Bacardi Squadron that day? In 1974, three CB radio operators appeared on a late-night TV

The Bermuda Triangle and Other Dangerous Polygons 115

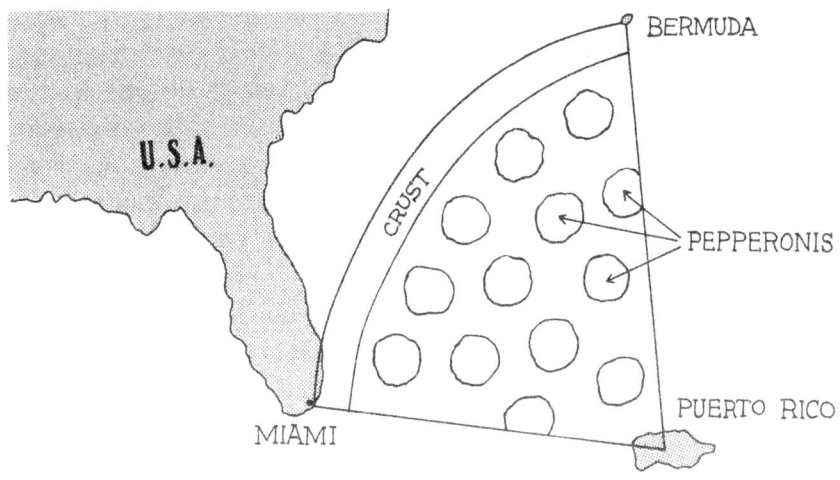

Figure 9B(2)
The Puerto Rican Pizza Slice

talk show claiming they had a tape recording of the last words from the missing squadron's flight leader. The men claimed they had intercepted the transmissions while testing their equipment in Key West on that fateful day in 1945. In front of a nationwide TV audience, they played their tape and revealed this amazing conversation:

Flight Leader: What is our position?

Navigator: We're sitting in our respective seats with our hands on our instruments.

Flight Leader: What are our coordinates, Bozo?

Navigator: Twenty-five degrees north of the equator on planet Earth.

Flight Leader: I know we're on planet Earth, dummy. Hey, what are those antennae doing on your head? You're not my navigator! AAAGGGHHH!

Navigator: Who do you think you're calling Bozo?

The CB operators said they had kept their tape recording a secret for all those years because they feared no one would believe them. After a poll was taken of the studio audience, it turned out that no one believed them anyway; they were thrown out and ended up selling their story to a tabloid newspaper, which published it next to some pictures from the television show "My Favorite Martian."

In any case, none of the men from the Bacardi Squadron were heard from again until thirty-two years later, when they showed up on the set of a Steven Spielberg movie. Even then no one had a chance to ask them about their disappearance, because they immediately joined Richard Dreyfuss in a spaceship that made loud farting noises and took off for another galaxy.

Did the Bacardi Squadron fly into a time warp used by UFOs to travel to our planet? If so, did the pilots have to reset their watches? These are just two of the many questions brought to mind by a lack of sleep while pondering the fate of these missing Avengers.

But the men of the Bacardi Squadron weren't the first to disappear in the Bermuda Triangle, just the ones most often exploited in books and articles about this mystery. The first people to disappear were probably the residents of the lost continent of Atlantis. Some archaeologists believe Atlantis once existed right at the center of the Bermuda Triangle, which may be why the continent suddenly vanished one day, wiping an entire civilization off the face of the earth. This would be quite a feat, considering that Atlantis was supposed to be the most highly advanced nation on the planet in its time. But that's only a theory; let's get back to the certified rumors.

Long before the Bacardi Squadron disappeared, the Bermuda Triangle was rumored by sailors to be a "graveyard of lost ships." Ever since Christopher Columbus first sailed through the region it has been known as a haunted sea, where the winds can suddenly come to a standstill, where miles of thick seaweed pervade the waters, and where Rod Serling and Alfred Hitchcock sometimes spent their vacations. There are literally scores of stories about ships and crews that were lost in the Bermuda Triangle; after researching these stories, I can testify that they are more than just fanciful fabrications. A lot of writers worked very hard to fabricate these tales. So make sure you appreciate them by getting scared when I summarize a few of them here.

On December 5, 1922, the cargo ship S.S. *Pyrolyte* left its port in Havana, Cuba, carrying six tons of nitroglycerine and an expert crew of chain-smoking sailors. The ship radioed back to shore twelve hours later to report that everything was "A-OK" as it sailed deeper and deeper into the Bermuda Triangle. That was the last anyone ever heard from the *Pyrolyte*. The vessel was reported missing two days later and the director of the Coast Guard ordered a comprehensive search for it. All ships that passed through the area where the *Pyrolyte* had been were thoroughly questioned, but none had made contact with the missing craft. Notably, several sailors said they had seen a bright flash in the vicinity; however, the investigators brushed this off as an unrelated incident. They assumed the flash was nothing more than lightning, or possibly a flying saucer crashing into the sea. After a search lasting several weeks, the *Pyrolyte* was finally given up for lost. It then became one of the hundreds of unexplained mysteries of the Bermuda Triangle.

Perhaps even more bizarre than ships and planes that vanish into thin air are the stories of ghost ships found wandering the seas after their crews have mysteriously vanished. Such was the case with the merchant ship *Derelictus*. On December 5, 1872, the *Derelictus* was spotted, listing badly as it sailed on an easterly course between the Azores and Portugal. Another merchant ship, the *Salvare*, pulled alongside the troubled vessel and sent a boarding party over to investigate. About an hour later, the boarding party reported back to the *Salvare*'s captain with an astounding story.

The ship was completely abandoned except for two cats, named Quake and Oats, who were known to be the mascots

118   Flying Saucers Are Everywhere

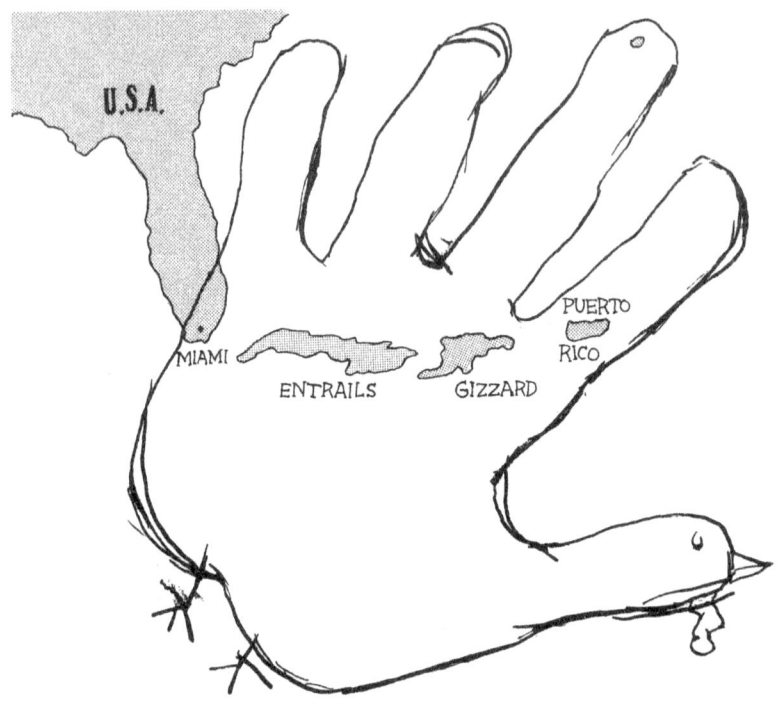

Figure 9B(3)
The North Atlantic Gobbler

of the missing crew. Mysteriously, a dinner of sauteed mackerel was still cooking on the stove when the *Salvare* party arrived, and the captain's dining table was primly set for two. It appeared that some of the ship's cargo of oatmeal had been thrown overboard, and one of the remaining crates was being used by the cats as a litter box.

Quake and Oats were well known to the crew of the *Salvare* and to many other people familiar with the *Derelictus*. When the *Derelictus* was in port, its crew would take Quake and Oats into pubs with them and entertain other sailors by showing them how the cats would eat oatmeal if they put a little catnip in it. Since oatmeal was usually the *Derelictus*' primary cargo, the crew didn't have to carry any catfood or pull in any fresh fish to feed their feline mascots.

The Bermuda Triangle and Other Dangerous Polygons   119

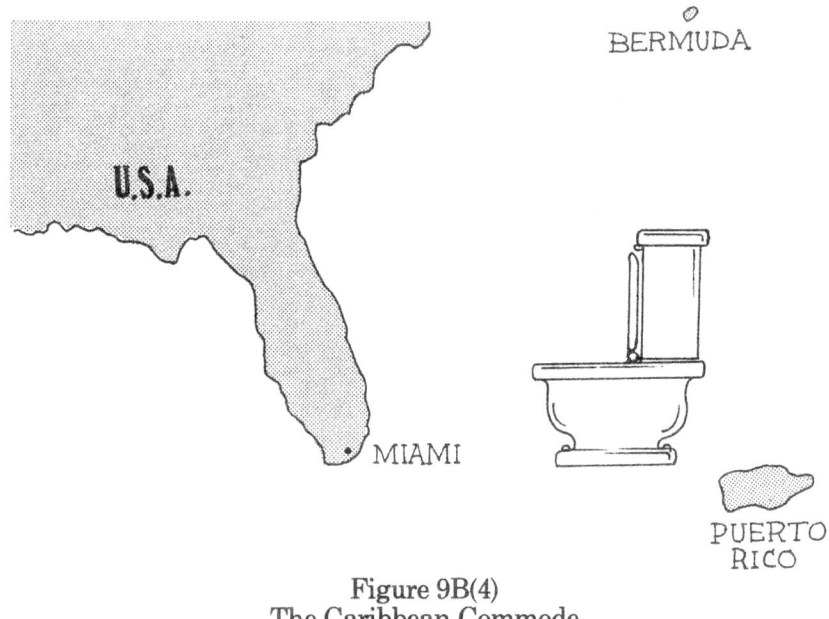

Figure 9B(4)
The Caribbean Commode

The crew of the *Salvare* put away the dinner dishes and brought the cats over to their ship, along with the remaining oatmeal. A tow was then attached to the *Derelictus* and the *Salvare* pulled it along on its journey toward Boston.

At this point, the mystery is compounded. For, a few days after it began towing the *Derelictus,* the *Salvare* was seen listing through the ocean as if it were in trouble. A British ship, the H.M.S. *Scuttlebutt,* attempted to communicate with it but couldn't find any signs of life on either ship, except for the two cats.

A boarding party from the *Scuttlebutt* reported back that they found no humans on board, only saw signs of a recently prepared fish dinner in the kitchen. The superstitious crew believed that the cats might be cursed, so they simply noted the encounter in the ship's log and continued on their way. When the *Scuttlebutt* reached port and notified the Coast Guard of their findings, they were told that several fishing boats had either vanished or been wrecked in the area where the two ghost ships had been seen.

Rumors began to spread on both sides of the Atlantic. Sailors would talk about the demon cats haunting the high seas while the government secretly worried about piracy and sabotage. The mystery was resolved two months later when a U.S. Navy spy boat spotted the two ghost ships 500 miles east of New York. Observers of the spy boat watched from a distance, as another Navy ship, disguised as a fishing boat, approached the two stray vessels.

Quake and Oats were seen dumping barrels of oatmeal into the ocean, right in the path of the undercover fishing boat. When it mixed with the water, the oatmeal congealed into gigantic lumps, which collided with the fishing boat and sank it on the spot. By the time the spy boat arrived, the two cats had rowed over to the fishing boat in a dinghy and stolen all their fish, leaving the crew to drown. The diabolical cats were arrested and court-martialed for piracy. They were found guilty and shot at sunrise the next day, after which their guts were used to make guitar strings.

On December 5, 1961, a new mystery was found floating in the Bermuda Triangle: an abandoned automobile. The shiny new Chevrolet was spotted by a Coast Guard Cutter, floating along on a calm, sunny day in the Caribbean, 100 miles south of Miami. The car's license plates were traced to a California man who said the car had a tendency to wander off on its own, but this was the first time it had ended up in the water. The perplexed owner flew to Miami to retrieve his vehicle and drove it back home, only to find that his house had drowned itself in the neighborhood swimming pool.

The disappearances haven't been stopped by modern technology either. On December 5, 1972, the nuclear-powered submarine U.S.S. *Crawdad* failed to arrive as scheduled at the Norfolk Naval Ship Yard. The last communication from the *Crawdad* had been a routine message that she was right on course and hadn't encountered any sea monsters. After pacing the docks for several hours, the admiral of the *Crawdad*'s fleet

The Bermuda Triangle and Other Dangerous Polygons   121

issued an all-points bulletin to find out what might have delayed the ship. All submarines and surface ships that passed anywhere near the *Crawdad*'s course were ordered to look around for the missing vessel.

Nothing was found until after nightfall, when the entire Atlantic Ocean began glowing bright yellow and radioactive jellyfish were seen flying through the air. The Navy was puzzled by this strange phenomenon; but when ocean temperatures reached the boiling point, a specialist suggested there might have been an accident with the *Crawdad*'s plutonium reactor. Temperatures eventually grew so hot that they warped the Bermuda Triangle into the shape of a large cheese wedge, which resulted in even more unexplained disappearances and caused a thin layer of mold to develop across the ocean's surface. Fortunately, the effect was only temporary. The triangle soon cooled back to its normal shape and 1973 turned out to be a banner year for the suppliers of radioactive penicillin.

Even supersonic jet aircraft have been spooked by anomalies in the triangle. On December 5, 1975, the Concorde SST was zooming across the triangle faster than the speed of sound when the pilot reported a near collision with something that had fallen out of the sky. Several ships were in the ocean below the jet and many of them saw the strange object as it plunged into the water. When the Coast Guard went out to investigate, they found an enormous chunk of floating ice. Everyone was baffled about how a chunk of ice could have fallen from outer space until lab tests identified it as "Gus" Shepard's frozen urine; its orbit had finally decayed, causing it to fall through the atmosphere from the previous chapter.

Mysterious disappearances are not just limited to the sea. As noted earlier, parts of the Bermuda Triangle are over land and many strange occurrences have happened there as well. The most famous of these cases was the lost colony of Roanoke, an island off the coast of North Carolina.

The Roanoke colony was founded by Sir Walter Raleigh, a wealthy tobacco magnate. After setting up the colony in 1587, Sir Walter decided to return to his home in England because there was rain in the forecast and he couldn't remember if he had left his windows open. Once home, Sir Walter was delayed by the discovery of an exceptionally good lager, so he didn't make it back to Roanoke until December 5, 1590. On his return, Sir Walter noted in his log that he was stunned by the peacefulness of the island. His sailors heard no sounds from the village when they approached and no one came to greet his ship when it landed.

Raleigh and his men entered the village where they found everything as they had left it three years before. The fort was still standing and the cabins were holding up quite well, but not a soul was there. It was as if the entire colony had been snatched into the sky by some unknown force.

What Sir Walter didn't tell anyone was that he had used the colony as collateral for a home equity loan made to him by some alien bankers. He had defaulted on the loan just before founding the colony, which is why he made up the phony excuse about leaving his windows open; he simply didn't want to be around when the aliens came to take possession. This little-known information was obtained from some very credible psychics who got in touch with the lost colonists a few years after their disappearance. The colonists said they had been treated very well by their captors and had finally taught the little men how to square dance. They reported that the aliens were still looking for Sir Walter because they thought if they could beam him into a pouch it would make for some hilarious tobacco jokes.

Disappearances continue to occur in the Bermuda Triangle at rates that are simply unmeasured, mainly because no one has bothered to measure them. What could possibly be causing all these ships, planes, cars, and people to vanish in ways that modern science can't explain? And why do all the disappearances occur on December 5? Is that the date on which the parallel universes line up, side by side, forming an interdimensional doorway in the Caribbean Sea? A doorway through which one can pass into an entirely new dimension, to meet with beings

The Bermuda Triangle and Other Dangerous Polygons   123

of a much higher intelligence, to travel in time as well as space? Or does that happen on April 5? I never was good with dates.

Anyway, the Bermuda Triangle isn't the only area in the world with an unusually high rate of disappearances. There are other zones scattered throughout the globe which, with a little imagination, can be construed as man-eating polygons that are just lying in wait for unsuspecting ships and planes to wander into their grasps. One of the more notorious of these is the Devil's Sea off the southeast coast of Japan (see Figure 9C).

On December 5, 1955, the Japanese government sent a research ship into the Devil's Sea to investigate some amazing claims that the place could be used as an Americanized tourist gimmick. The expedition obtained funding from American research groups interested in a possible link between this Japanese Sea and the Bermuda Triangle, which is on the exact opposite side of the earth. The project's ship, the *Amerikaro* (roughly translates to: sucker Americans), was outfitted with the most expensive surveillance equipment available at the time, all of it made in Japan.

As soon as the *Amerikaro* entered the boundaries of the Devil's Sea, the crew sent out an SOS saying their ship was sinking and had to be abandoned. By the time a rescue ship arrived, the entire crew was in lifeboats and the *Amerikaro* had mysteriously exploded. The daring Japanese tried to get funding for two more research vessels but their financiers refused to let them risk their lives again. Instead, they published a series of paperback books and documentary films about other ships that had been sucked into the Devil's Sea so hard that they left no record of having ever even existed.

In addition to the Devil's Sea, there are at least five other mystery zones known to the followers of anomalous polygons. These are shown on the following maps.

In the Falkland Islands there is an area known as the Falkland Funnel (figure 9D), where sailors who stay too long have been known to abandon their ships, disrobe on the beach, and dance naked among the penguins.

In the jungle of Madagascar there is the Madagascar Moon

Figure 9C

Pie (figure 9E), an area shaped like a moon pie with a bite taken out of it. Anyone who enters this territory loses his hat, and can only get it back by tracking down a clan of native squirrel monkeys and defeating the dominant male in a dung-throwing contest.

In eastern Russia there is a place called the Siberian Spiral (figure 9F). All currency that enters this troubled zone completely vanishes, or, even worse, is converted into rubles at the official exchange rate.

The Bermuda Triangle and Other Dangerous Polygons 125

In western Australia there is the Octagon Down Under (figure 9G), where cars break down for no apparent reason, and the occupants are drop-kicked into the desert by wild kangaroos.

And at the Municipal Golf Course in Poolesville, Maryland, there is the Poolesville Pentagon (figure 9H), an area of thick bushes outside the dogleg on the first hole, which sucks up millions of golf balls each year, none of which are ever seen again on this earth.

Obvious connections exist between flying saucers and the seven mystery zones we've discussed here. For one, books on both topics are always kept in the same section of the library. In addition, almost every book on the Bermuda Triangle has a chapter on UFOs and, as demonstrated here, UFO books always include a chapter on the triangle mystery. Moreover, the frequency of flying saucer reports in all seven mystery zones has been found to be directly proportional to the number of Bermuda Triangle books sold at local bookstores. Let's look at a simple equation to see how this works.

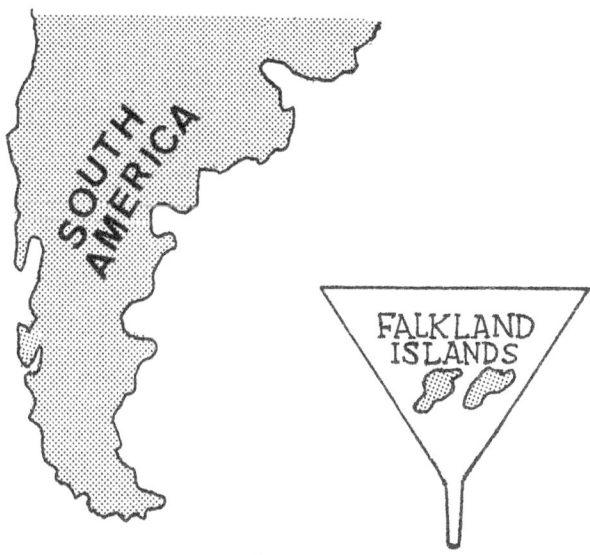

Figure 9D
The Falklands Funnel

126 Flying Saucers Are Everywhere

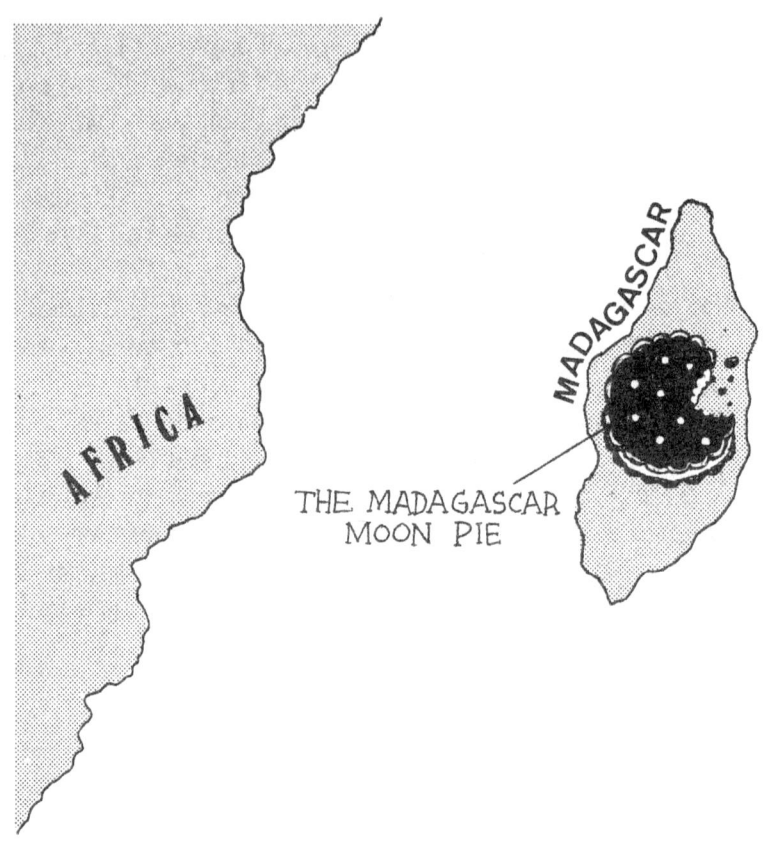

Figure 9E

$$Sk^{UFO} = BC$$

The **S** in this equation is the number of flying saucer sightings in a given area over some fixed period of time. **B** is the number of books about the Bermuda Triangle that have been sold in that area over the same time period. **C** is the number of flying saucer books sold. **k** is known as the kook factor. The value of **k** varies considerably, but it seems to be especially high at the full moon and during times of military and economic tension. The ^{UFO} has no particular meaning in this equation;

The Bermuda Triangle and Other Dangerous Polygons 127

Figure 9F
The Siberian Spiral

it was just added for special effect. This equation clearly demonstrates that no matter what causes the mysterious phenomena in the Bermuda Triangle, flying saucer book sales would be in serious trouble without a substantial kook factor.

128 Flying Saucers Are Everywhere

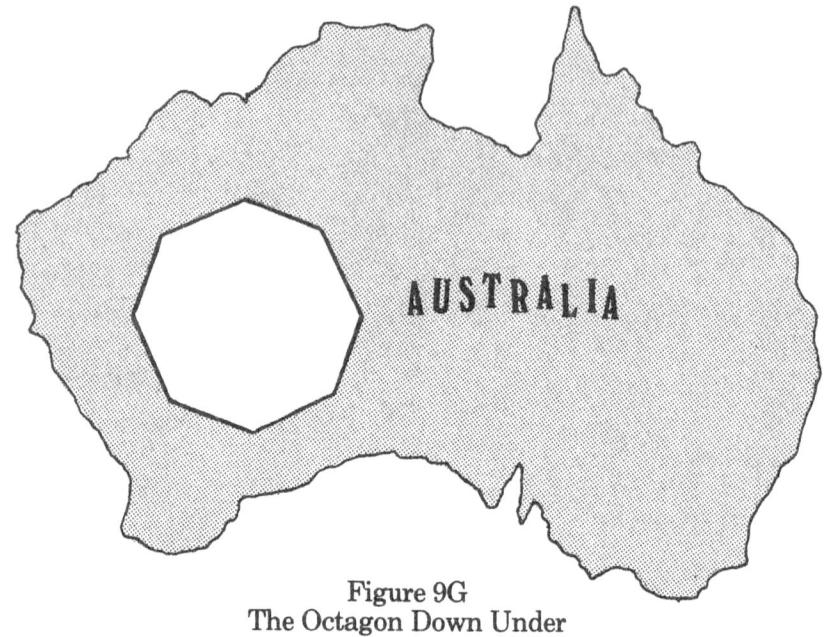

Figure 9G
The Octagon Down Under

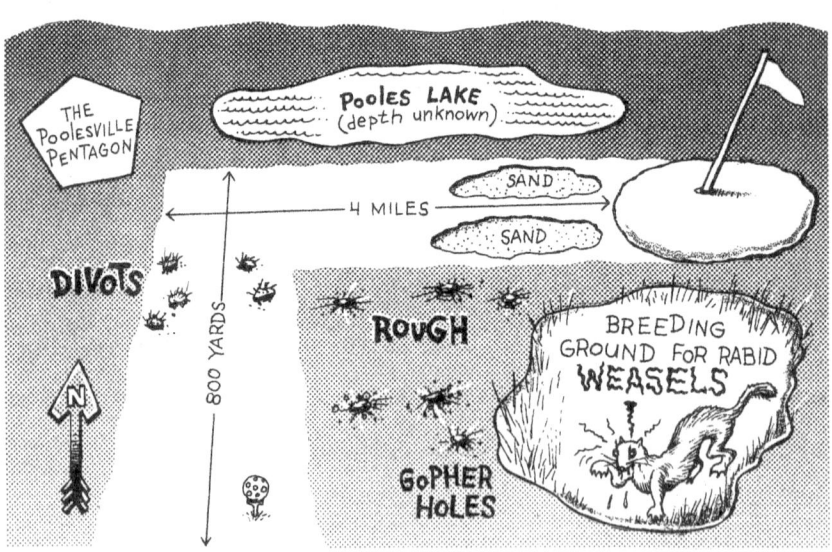

Figure 9H

Ten

Flying Saucers in the World Today

Now it is time to assess the situation of flying saucers in the world today. As this book goes to print, a major UFO flap is underway in Western Europe. The Western Europeans may not be aware of this yet, but they'll hear about it soon; the story has just broken on a Fox TV special sponsored by Miller Genuine Draft. The center of this UFO activity, according to the show's narrator, is in Brussels, Belgium, which happens to be the seat of the European Parliament. This could mean that the aliens want to become trading partners with the newly unified Europe, or it could simply indicate their fondness for the native Brussels sprouts.

The most common language in Belgium is Flemish, so called because its deep, guttural sounds sometimes cause the speaker to cough up "flem" in mid-sentence. The Flemish word for flying saucer is totally unpronounceable, in fact, scores of people have actually died trying to pronounce it, which may be why so few flying saucer witnesses have come forward in Belgium even during the current wave of activity.

The Diligent Organization for the Research of Flying Saucers (DORFS) once formed a chapter in Brussels, but all its members died during their first meeting in a tragic case of mass gagging. Fortunately, the Belgians are able to communicate in writing about flying saucers by using the English acronym UFO. The corresponding Flemish abbreviation could be used, but Belgian publishers fear that printing it might tempt readers to try to pronounce the letters, and that, too, could be fatal.

Another wave of UFO sightings has been reported in South America this year, where UFOs are called "OVNI." This Spanish acronym, which stands for *Objectos Voladores No Identificados,* has caused some confusion in the press because it is also an affectionate nickname for obese women (as in "My, what a large *posterioro* you're getting, my dear *ovni*"). This misunderstanding led an American tabloid to print, as its headline, late last year, "Argentine Women Become Airborne After Eating Too Many Soybeans." Argentine women haven't really become airborne by themselves, but a few of them have reported being abducted by the UFOs.

In the United States, the current hotbed of UFO activity is Gulf Breeze, Florida. It was here in 1993 that hundreds of witnesses watched and photographed a UFO as it hovered above the beach for hours before being accidentally snagged by a fisherman whose line got tangled up with it. Faithful believers insist that just because the Gulf Breeze aliens travel in cardboard spaceships only one foot in diameter, this does not mean they aren't a highly advanced race. In fact, the Gulf Breeze aliens, which still hover nightly over crowds of tourists, appear to be very considerate of our earthly environment; all their spaceships are made from recycled milk cartons.

So, clearly the UFOs are with us today as much as they have always been. The questions we need to ask now are: Where do they come from? What are their intentions? And what sort of wild speculations can we indulge in about their future?

From what the contactees have told us, there appears to be a great variety of aliens from many different parts of the universe visiting Earth. The Bumpkins, for example, were abducted by beings from Beta Gesticulate and Herman Schizmann's aliens came all the way from another galaxy.

Given the large number of alien species visiting our planet, one may conclude that the earth is a major stopping point for intergalactic travelers, a cosmic truck stop so to speak. This theory is not inconsistent with the revelations of an alien named FOBS, who has been communicating with earthlings for over twenty years through psychic Jerry Fourflusher of Humbug, West Virginia. FOBS has dictated several volumes of cosmic revelations through Fourflusher, some of which can be construed to agree with my own theories of how the aliens view our popular planet. In a recent interview I asked FOBS why our planet was such a common stopping place. This was his response:

> The first aliens began coming to Earth before life evolved because it was such a peaceful, rustic place to get away from the hustle and bustle of intergalactic commerce. The discoveries of things like a 2-billion-year-old battery by your archaeologists are traces of those prehistoric alien visits. The battery, for example, was probably left by an alien family on a camping trip during these early times.
>
> Later, Earth became popular as an entertainment planet; beings would come from light years around to watch the development of mankind. Humans are a very entertaining species to most aliens because they are so physically durable and adaptable; yet they haven't learned how to levitate. It is hilarious for us to watch you invent clumsy, heavier-than-air planes and powerful jet engines when you would be able to fly much more efficiently if you could only learn how to meditate at the right frequencies. This might be analogous to the amusement humans get from watching a dog chase its tail.

Next, I asked FOBS if any of the alien species frequenting our planet were interbreeding with humans.

> As you know, many contactees, under hypnosis, have told stories of copulating with aliens during their abduction. Your UFOlogists have theorized that this is because the aliens are sterile and need the assistance of a relatively young species

like humans to help them reproduce, but this is only part of the story. It is true that many alien species like the "Cricket Men" are sterile, and that they have succeeded in creating half-breeds with human abductees. But the main reason for aliens copulating with human beings has been the fascination they have for your sex counselor Dr. Ruth Westheimer.

The Cricket Men and other sterile aliens are all sufficiently advanced to reproduce through cloning, but after Dr. Ruth's Video Guide to Good Sex was published extraterrestrially by Globular Cluster Communications, these species began to feel they were missing out on something by reproducing without sex. Dr. Ruth's guide has shattered records throughout the known universe for video cassette sales, even surpassing *E.T.* on most planets.

FOBS' answer explains why some victims of UFO abductions have told of being quizzed by the aliens about "foreplay" and "afterglow." It also explains a very strange abduction case reported in Missouri where the aliens asked the victim to wear a blue skirt and speak with a squeaky voice and a German accent.

I also asked FOBS if any of the aliens had plans to take over any part of the earth against the will of its inhabitants.

This has been tried many times by a variety of different species. The latest effort was an attempt by a consortium of aliens to take over the Cable News Network and put it out of business. They wanted to do this because the continuous stream of international crises and third-rate commercials broadcast into the atmosphere was interfering with their anti-gravity propulsion systems. The takeover was called off, however, after a technician figured out how to circumvent the interference by installing a 200-channel remote control device on every spaceship. This has proved 95 percent effective against the interference except on New Years Day, when the predominance of bowl games on all channels forces most saucers to remain in their hangars until the final coaches' poll is released.

Flying Saucers in the World Today 133

Finally, I asked FOBS if he could tell us when the aliens would make themselves known to the general public instead of just abducting and communicating with selected earth people. His answer to this surprised me.

> Soon after your book is published, there will be such a deluge of sightings in all parts of your planet that no one will doubt that flying saucers are real. At that time your politicians will be forced to reveal all they know, and aliens will begin to communicate openly with your mass media, answering many of your questions about us, such as why I always speak in inset paragraphs. All these things will occur by the middle of next year.

So, if FOBS is correct, the publication of this book will trigger a worldwide flap of flying saucer sightings, and by the middle of next year all our questions about flying saucers should be answered. Of course, if FOBS is wrong, then we'll know that Mr. Fourflusher, like many people before him, has been pulling one over on all of us.

Whatever the case, the faithful followers of the flying saucer phenomenon believe that we now stand at the threshold of a new phase in the evolution of mankind. They point to the rapid increase of unearthly phenomena in recent years, like the crop circles, the Swiss holes, the increase in UFO activity, and the emergence of white rap singers. Saucer enthusiasts say that these are all signs of an impending scientific, technologic, and psychoneurotic breakthrough that will lift mankind into a new dimension of knowledge and spirituality. And, since these same enthusiasts spend a large percentage of their disposable income on flying saucer books, I'm inclined to agree with them.

But seriously, all we need to do is look at the newspaper or television to see that we are going through a period of rapid change in our culture. A scant ten years ago no one would have dreamed that peace treaties would be signed in all the world's major trouble spots, let alone that these events would have to compete for news coverage with a penis mutilation trial.

And just a decade ago UFOlogists were predicting that mass landings and open communications with aliens would occur within five years. Today we're saying they will occur within a year. Miraculous progress can be seen all around us. From the collapse of communism to the demise of common discretion, we see signs of a world that is struggling to shrug off its old cocoon so it can evolve into its next phase of development.

But what is that next phase and where will it lead us? Will we finally learn the secrets of the aliens' space drive and become a new partner in intergalactic trade? Will we make incredible new medical breakthroughs and find a better material for breast implants? Will we learn to travel forward and backward in time so we can bankrupt Las Vegas by betting on past Superbowls? The possibilities are as endless as the universe.

And what about our relationship with the aliens? Will they stop abducting us surreptitiously and start treating us as equals for a change? Or will they enslave us and use us as cheap, primate laborers to fulfill their imperialistic designs and their sexual fantasies? And will Princess Diana finally divorce her husband and run off with Elvis Presley?

I'm afraid I'm not able to answer all of these provocative questions as easily as I'm able to ask them. I know I sort of promised to blow the lid off this whole flying saucer thing at the beginning of the book, but it turns out to be even more complicated than I thought, and besides, I have to save something for a sequel.

But maybe we're better off not knowing all the answers right now. Maybe it's not so important what the answers are as long as we catch people's attention, as long as we stimulate their gullible imaginations and lure them into the bookstores looking for answers. For, as any true devotee of the flying saucer phenomenon knows, every answer we find only serves to generate more and more questions, producing a need for more and more research, resulting in more and more theories, and leading to the sales of more and more UFO books.

As a dedicated UFOlogist, I'm willing to put up with all these uncertainties. I'm willing to fly around the world as long as it takes, asking bizarre questions and searching for illusory answers. I'm willing to continue accepting exorbitant fees for delivering sensationalist lectures and to keep up with the latest cult fads by publishing as many books as my little fingers can type up. So, as long as you trusting readers keep your vivid imaginations oiled, I'll do my part and keep discovering, exposing, and inventing more intriguing cosmic mysteries that you and I, together, can try to solve.

God, I love this business!

www.ingramcontent.com/pod-product-compliance
Lightning Source LLC
Chambersburg PA
CBHW051449290426
44109CB00016B/1688